International Business Communication

Global Communicator's Handbook

Preeti Oza

ATLANTIC
PUBLISHERS & DISTRIBUTORS (P) LTD

ATLANTIC
PUBLISHERS & DISTRIBUTORS (P) LTD

7/22, Ansari Road, Darya Ganj, New Delhi
Tel.: +91-11-4077 5252, 2327 3880
E-mail: orders@atlanticbooks.com
Web: www.atlanticbooks.com

Published by Atlantic Publishers & Distributors (P) Ltd 2024

Printed & bound in India by Atlantic Print Services

To two gentlemen who are my heroes,
mentors, and biggest supporters.
The first one is Prof. Dr. Ramesh Oza,
my Father-in-law, whose encouragement
was my fuel and who has made me
what I am today.
The second one is
Shree Kanak Chandra Bhatt,
my father, whose wisdom has been
my compass and who taught me
the true meaning of strength
and integrity.

Preface

In today's ever-more-interconnected world, effective international corporate communication is more important than ever. Effective communication is necessary whenever one is attempting to conduct business with a customer located on the opposite side of the world or when one is working with a coworker who hails from a foreign country. This book looks at the condition of communication as it is today as well as the shifts that have occurred in business communication. Even though we are primarily concerned with businesses, the fundamental ideas may just as easily be applied to charitable organisations, the voluntary sector, as well as small, medium and big businesses. It is impossible to exaggerate the significance of communication in international business transactions. If you don't use global communication effectively, you can end up creating more issues than it solves. This is something that needs to be taken into consideration very seriously when negotiating contracts across different cultures and languages. It is the responsibility of the organisation to make certain that its employees have access to the tools necessary for efficient communication.

Variations in national character, noise across cultural boundaries and the translation of language are the three obstacles that need to be conquered. It is important to gain an understanding of a variety of cultures and to ensure that your team includes at least one member who is conversant in the language as well as the culture with which you will be interacting. The only difference between traditional business communication and international business communication is that the latter transcends cultural barriers, while the former does not. Having noted that, it becomes challenging as there are substantial variations in cultural norms and expectations among different nations. Communication across international boundaries can be made more difficult by factors, such as the use of technology, variations in culture and language hurdles. Yet, these barriers may be conquered with some careful planning, some guidance from an expert and a fundamental understanding of the concepts behind effective cross-cultural communication. This will allow international business relationships to be carried out successfully. Effective communication is more vital than it has ever been in today's global economy, in which companies of all sizes are in direct competition with one another for customers and business. According to the findings of one survey, employees in 25 percent of all jobs are required to communicate with people from foreign nations.

Communication is essential in the setting of a business corporation for two reasons. To begin, it makes it less difficult for you to comprehend people who come from different cultural backgrounds and to communicate with them. It is crucial to grasp and accept cultural variations while working with customers or coworkers from different countries. These people may be from a different country. To be able to work effectively with them, you need to first understand their perspectives, actions and preferred modes of communication before you can develop the necessary communication skills. Second, having the ability to communicate in a few different languages is absolutely necessary in today's global market. If you are marketing to a new international audience but are unable to interact with your clients in their native tongue, you run the risk of losing out on large prospects that competitors are using. Another key element is culture. You will eventually be forced to deal with international business communication if you are a businessperson who has many clients located in other countries, an expat who works in global management or both. The modern-day corporate climate places a large emphasis on the importance of cultural diversity. Regardless of whether you own a small business or a huge corporation, it is vital that you understand and respect the customs and values of your customers and employees. To accomplish this goal, you will need to devise a strategy for communicating across cultural boundaries. This guide will give you with the information and skills you need to improve the operations of your company and demonstrate the unique values that your customers and workers bring to the table. You may build a successful worldwide organisation by first gaining an awareness of and then embracing the cultural differences that exist among your customers and staff. This book goes over some of the most important strategies that may be used for effective communication in international business.

Acknowledgements

I am incredibly grateful to everyone who has contributed to this amazing adventure as I think back on the process of making this book come to reality. I want to start by sincerely thanking my family, whose constant support and faith in my goal have been the cornerstones of my resiliency and willpower. I want to thank my parents for teaching me the importance of perseverance and hard work. My heartfelt gratitude goes out to my editor Ms. Chitra Lele whose perceptive observations and exacting attention to detail have allowed my work to reach its greatest potential. Her commitment to excellence and professionalism is immeasurable. My sincere appreciation goes out to the amazing team at Atlantic Publishers, particularly to Ms. Namarita and the marketing and sales personnel, who have dedicated many hours to bringing this book to the attention of readers. I have been inspired and motivated by the team's passion and dedication. I am grateful to the academic and professional communities for their research and educational contributions. Their insights have played a crucial role in enhancing the quality of my book and provided the basis for my own research. Lastly, I would like to thank you, my dear reader, for joining me on this voyage. Through our mutual love of the topic, this book serves as both a discourse and a reflection of my passion and dedication. I appreciate your interest and involvement, and for letting my words enter your space.

With sincere gratitude,

Dr. Preeti Oza

List of Figures

Contents

Part V: Effective Written Communication in International Business

Part VI: Oral Communication Skills for Global Business

Part VII: Technology in International Business Communication

Part VIII: Building and Maintaining International Business Relationships

Part IX: Managing Conflicts and Ethical Dilemmas in International Business

Part I

Introduction to International Business Communication

1

Defining International Business Communication

Introduction

The origin of the English term 'communication' can be traced back to the Latin term 'Communis'. Communis translates to the word 'common' and this word encapsulates the actions of creating, transmitting, engaging in, or distributing shared or common content or elements. It is a procedure where evidence, concepts and views are exchanged for a person or company to express meaning and comprehend each other. Across other aspects, it involves interaction and communication of information comprising realities, beliefs, opinions, feelings and mind-sets. The advancement of humanity has indeed been facilitated by the capacity to interact between frontiers and all over cultures. The capacity to facilitate quick and efficient communications across borders has lowered distances and brought 'global capitalism' into being. Communication seemed necessary to ensure that members of one nation, civilization or linguist community interacted and related with members of certain other nations, civilizations or linguist communities. Life on this earth acquires relevance only through communicating. It promotes affection and comprehension and aids in relation development. It broadens the understanding of the cosmos and enhances the value of life.

Significance of Communication in Business

Every conversation that people convey or get for administrative purposes, such as operating a business, management of the company, official activities of a non-profit organisation, and so on is referred to as international business communication.

Compared to interpersonal and societal correspondence, international business communication is characterised by formalism.

All firms' ability to communicate effectively and efficiently is a major factor that determines their achievement. It occurs between business enterprises, markets and market locations, inside of organisations, different groups of the workforce, leaders and staff, purchasers and sellers, key suppliers and clients, sales representatives and prospects, and between individuals within the organisation and the press. These communications affect business. When handled carefully, these interactions could advance commercial objectives. If not, it would reflect poorly on the company and harm business interests. According to Pumble (it is a free business messaging app), teams, who communicate effectively in the workplace may see as much as a 25% increase in their productivity. On the other hand, Project co's (it is a client portal for service businesses) Communication Statistics 2023 report highlighted that the costs of poor business communication include:

- Wasted time (according to 68%),
- Missed messages (53%),
- Burnout, stress and fatigue (42%),
- Lost files (35%),
- Bad customer experience (30%),
- Lost customers to competitors (12%), and
- Lost employees (10%).

Every foundation's communication system has always been its lifeline, which primarily serves to bring about transformation and conduct. Managing an efficient method of communication is a fundamental challenge in every firm. Deprived communication is typically the outcome of operational issues. Commands are misinterpreted, which leads to major errors. The fundamental issue with communicating is that what has been genuinely comprehended might differ from what the other person meant to say. The communication passed between the speaker and the listening person could well be distorted by various factors, because they are two independent people with distinct limits.

Interior communication happens, when individuals inside an enterprise interact with one another. They do this to collaborate and achieve their shared objectives. It might be authorised or prohibited. Frontal and writing modes are both forms of communication occurring internally. Instances of interior communication include memoranda, documents, office orders, circulars, faxes, video-conferences, global meetings, and so on.

Exterior communication is the exchange of information between organisational members and anybody from outside. Such persons could be users or consumers, traders or suppliers, the press, the government or the broader community.

- Communication is essential to the operation of every company. Without an efficient communication infrastructure, none of the firms might grow.
- Regardless of the type of business or magnitude, communication seems to be the foundation that keeps an organisation intact.
- Communication occurs internally, when individuals inside an organisation speak with one another, whereas exterior communication happens, when individuals inside an organisation speak with anyone outside the organisation.
- Effective communication is essential for teamwork, managing coworkers, and maintaining relationships with superiors, clients and teammates.

Research carried out by McKinsey (it is a worldwide management consulting firm) shows that well-connected teams can increase their productivity by 20 to 25%. Further research was undertaken by Think Talent (it is focussed on recruitment of engineering, mining and technical professionals) and CMS Wire (it is the leading publication covering digital customer experience methodologies, tools and operations) and it shows that organisations with effective communication strategies were 3.5 times more likely to outperform their peers

Definitions of Communication

Communication can be described as the exchange of ideas or data among two or more people to promote co-operative comprehension and the intended activity. It entails the sharing of data through symbolism or words. The commonality of passion, goal and endeavour is produced by the sharing of information, opinions and perspectives.

Communication is defined by the American Managerial Association as "all activities that result in an interchange of meanings".

According to Peter Little, communication is the procedure whereby data is exchanged among people and/or organisations to produce a comprehensible reply.

Communication is defined by Newman and Summer Jr. as an interchange of evidence, thoughts, views or attitudes by two or more people.

As per Keith Davis, 'Communication is a process of passing information and understanding from one person to another'. In essence, it serves as a bridge of meanings for the population. One could securely traverse the stream of miscommunication by utilizing the bridging aspect.

According to Louis A. Allen, communicating is the summation of every action an individual performs to foster comprehension in the minds of others. It entails a methodical, ongoing trend of communicating by speaking, hearing and comprehending.

As a result, the major goal of communication is to enlighten and persuade others to adopt a particular viewpoint or motivate them to take action.

Features of Communication

- Fundamentally, communicating is a two-sided procedure. The input we receive determines whether the communication is successful or unsuccessful. Feedback is therefore pivotal to interaction.
- Throughout all managerial levels along with all types of companies, communicating is a continual activity that is vital. None of the supervisors can do her or his duties effectively, if they are unable to interact. Companies that value professionalism and results are constantly searching for executives with strong communication skills.

- In communication, thoughts and sentiments are just as important as facts. Sayings alone are only a tiny part of communication. More messages are frequently conveyed via tone and facial gestures than through speech. With signals, symbolism and movements, one could convey a lot. A 2-fingered triumph sign, for instance, communicates more effectively than speech.
- The method of communicating is versatile. It takes into account how the shapes of performers as well as the atmosphere are altering.
- It is a procedure with objectives. When the recipient and sender are indeed conscious of the communication's aim and that the purpose is coherent, collaborating can be productive.
- Communication is a multi-disciplinary field of study wherein, experience gained across multiple disciplines is being utilised. Understanding how people communicate effectively has been assisted by anthropological research (the science of body language), psychological (the science of persuading, cognition and beliefs), sociological (the science of human society) and political discipline (the science of voting trends).

Goals of Communication

The following is a list of primary intentions or purposes of communication:

Guidance

The authoritative aspect is a constant theme in the instructive role. It has a rather directive character. As a result, the interpreter provides a subsequent step with essential instructions and directions to allow a person to carry out her or his specific job. Here, guidelines generally go from the upper phase to the lesser phase.

Incorporation

It is a condensed activity whereby efforts are made to integrate operations. The primary goal of communication is to establish relationships between several business organisational functionalities. It aids in the fusion of several managerial tasks.

To provide information

In an enterprise, communication serves the objective of informing a person or a group regarding a specific assignment, business policies, processes, and so on. Through the medium level, the top managing system communicates policy to the lower level. The medium level then communicates the lower level's response to the top level. Information may move in vertical, horizontal and diagonal ways throughout the organisation. The basic goal of communicating is to update oneself or someone else.

Appraisal

Communication is the process by which actions are examined to generate ideas or render judgments about the value of an activity. A strategy for evaluating the contribution of a person or a team to the organisation is communication. A suitable and efficient communication method is required for assessing one's input, outcomes of others or even a few ideologies framework.

Direction

Upper executives or a supervisor must communicate with lower levels to give them instructions. Once workers receive guidance from a superior, they will function best. Written or verbal communication can be used to lead each other. Conventional orders, requests orders and inferred orders are various types of orders.

Educating

It has been widely accepted how important workplace safeguarding is. A thorough communication approach is necessary to train and instruct employees concerning individual security at work. The workforce could save costs, processes, risks and other issues by communicating effectively.

Impacting

A thorough communication strategy is required while attempting to persuade someone or when being impacted. A person with the power to affect somebody could readily convince everyone else. It alludes to the giving of a response that reveals the results of the interaction.

To create an image

A company cannot exist in isolation from the remainder of the societal structure. Civilization and a business entity working in society are interconnected as well as dependent on one another. Community assurance and trust must inevitably be built. It may be accomplished through interactions with several sources that must represent the company's image in society. An organisation's role is to tell the public about its objectives, initiatives, advancements, and societal responsibilities across an efficient exterior communication network.

Relating to staff configuration

When a new staff member joins a company, she or he won't be familiar with its norms, procedures, cultures, and so on. Employees can become more familiar with their superiors, coworkers and the company's practices, goals, laws and regulations by receiving timely communication about all these aspects.

Others

Whenever the decision-maker is given the necessary and sufficient knowledge, efficient decision-making is feasible. Creating decisions is made easier, when there is good communication. To do duties successfully and efficiently, each person in the business must usually give pertinent details.

Situations of Communication

Whenever there is a communication situation,

- Someone (the sender or transmitter) wishes to transfer certain info
- The information must be communicated to another individual (the recipient)
- The message conveyed to the recipient is partially or fully understood by her or him
- The communication is returned or feedback is received from the recipient

These four elements are necessary for effective communication.

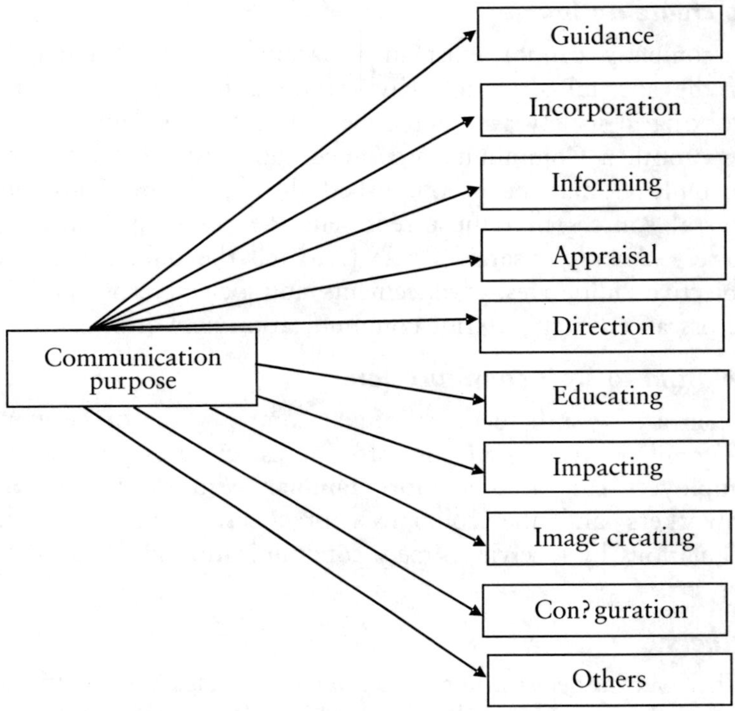

Figure 1.1: Intention of Communication
Source: https://www.researchgate.net/figure/Purpose-of-Communication-10-Other-Effective-decision-making-is-possible-when-required_fig1_367964407

Importance of Communication

Success in business is often dependent on effective communication. Because of the following factors, communication has subsequently become even more vital:

Size expansion

The size of business organisations has significantly increased. These days, a huge corporation offers opportunities to numerous employees to operate all over the globe. For the successful completion of its tasks, an effective communication system is necessary.

Rising Specialisation

Rigid job segmentation causes various tasks to be performed by multiple agencies. An organisation cannot run efficiently, when there is a lack of effective interaction between the various sections to ensure mutual understanding and collaboration. For instance, if the manufacturing and marketing divisions of the organisation are unable to communicate, the sales force may place an order that the manufacturing department is unable to accomplish.

Increasingly fierce competitiveness

Due to liberalisation and globalisation, there is competitive pressure between domestic and international banks. To thrive in the battle of competitiveness, persuasion communication through commercials and personal as well as public interactions will turn out to be important.

Trade unity movement

Employee unions seem to be extremely powerful and influential in enterprises. Along with several issues, the management should engage union representatives. Managerial and union representatives can preserve positive relationships by regularly exchanging information and ideas.

Interpersonal relationships

Establishing faith and confidence mutually amongst the workforce and managers necessitates good communication. The involvement of staff in decision-making and other operations fosters a feeling of commitment and connection across them to the company.

Public affairs

The community demands that executives behave responsibly. Businesses must educate the governments, customers, providers, shareholders, and other societal groups concerning their social contributions. Large corporations use specialised professionals for public affairs to assist in business boost and societal reputation.

Personal strength

Effective communication is crucial for gaining achievements in each profession. Executives need to give talks, produce documentation and arrange interview sessions. Reception staff, instructors, lawyers and defenders require having great communication skills.

The Process or Cycle of Communication

The communication process is made up of the sender's thoughts being transmitted to the recipient and the recipient's response to the sender. Whenever an individual (the sender) wishes to convey facts, concepts, viewpoints or other information to another individual (the recipient), communication is said to have commenced. The sender does have a purpose for such information, concepts or viewpoints. The message must then be converted or translated into a language that accurately expresses the concept. So, the message needs to be encrypted. The substance of the message, the level of acquaintance of both sender and recipient, as well as other circumstances significantly affect the encoding process.

The message is delivered through the proper network or media after having been encrypted. Conferences, reporting, memoranda, notes, e-mails, faxes and telephone conversations are frequent communication channels in organisations. When a message is obtained, it is decrypted by the recipient, who then informs the sender of whether the message has indeed been properly understood.

Communication Components

The following components are a part of the communication procedure:

Sender or broadcaster

A sender, also referred to as a broadcaster, is the individual, who wants to communicate the message. The messaging is started by a sender, who also modifies the recipient's conduct.

Message

It is a topic that is covered in all communications. Every fact, thought, viewpoint or informational element might be included. If communication is to occur, it should present within the thoughts of the sender.

Encrypting

The information presenter arranges her or his thought into a collection of symbols (phrases, signs, and so on) that she or he believes it will get transmitted to the targeted recipient in an effective manner.

Stream of communicating

The sender must choose the route to transmit the data. The medium used for communicating is the medium by which the message travels. It serves as the channel between the sender and the recipient.

Recipient

The recipient of a communication is referred to as the receiver or perhaps the individual to whom the transmitter sends a certain statement. If one is deprived of the presence of the intended recipient, it is impossible to communicate. An individual, who gets and attempts to comprehend the communication is the recipient.

Decryption

It is the method of translating information that has been encrypted into its clear meaning. The recipient can extract meaning from a statement with the aid of decryption.

Feedback

Communication is a method of exchanging information. For the interchange to be accomplished, the sender (or the person, who sent the basic data) should obtain the returned information such that she or he may learn how the recipient responded. Feedback is the term for the recipient's reaction or response.

Brain drains

It is the term used to describe the probability of misconceptions at any stage during the entire process. This might occur on behalf of the sender if they select the default stream to convey the message rather than selecting an appropriate media. It could also occur, if the recipient improperly decodes the message. In other terms, one might claim that any phase of the cycle has been broken.

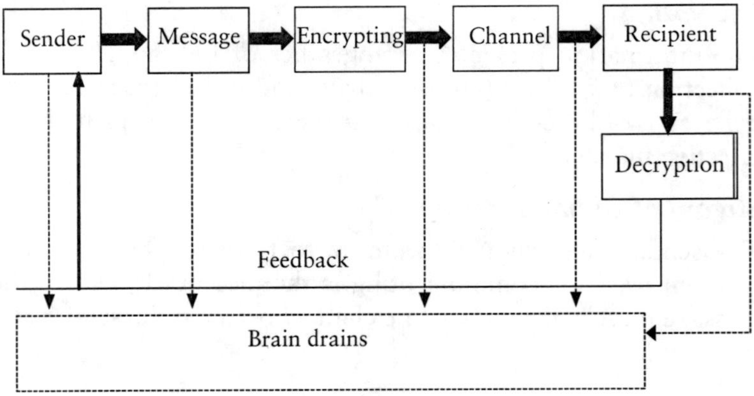

Figure 1.2: Process of Communication

Source: https://www.researchgate.net/figure/The-Communication-Process_fig2_367964407

The term 'communication' is rooted in the Latin word 'communis' and it pertains to the sharing of information for shared understanding. In business, it's vital for success but faces challenges from operational issues.

Multidisciplinary and goal-oriented, communication fosters productivity and performance. Key goals include guidance, incorporation, providing information and influencing. Business success depends on effective communication due to size expansion, specialization, competitiveness, trade unions, interpersonal relationships and public affairs. The communication process involves a sender, message, encoding, communication channel, recipient, decoding and feedback. Misunderstandings or brain drains stress the importance of selecting appropriate communication media.

Activity

1. How would you describe communication?
2. How does communication play a part in business management?
3. What are the various goals does communication serve?
4. Communicating is the sharing of information, thoughts, feelings and views between two or more individuals. Discuss the meaning of this statement and the function of feedback in communication.

5. Communication is a two-sided process. Justify.
6. Explain the various components of communication.
7. Discuss the importance of proper encoding and decoding in ensuring effective communication.
8. List 3 instances of brain drain that occur in the communication process.

2

Global Business Environment

Introduction

Even in local business, where a company must cope with matters, such as taxes and policies, shifts in the financial system, competitive risks, political variables, administration rules, industrial authorizations, environmental issues, legal adherence to various acts and rules and keeping up with the rapidly evolving technical landscape, the company has no control over the outside world. When a company expands into foreign markets, it must cope with distinct business environments in the new nations, which makes things very complicated. The phrase 'the total of all the exterior forces functioning upon the company as it goes about its affairs in the international marketplace refers to the dynamics of the global business environment. Given that executives are knowledgeable about the local business environment and the variables that shape it such as the political economy, a company can devise an approach of activity for handling unpredictable external variables.

This isn't the case for global corporate operations as they are subject to numerous unavoidable external variables. These difficulties include, but are not limited to, unclear foreign trade regulations, shifting political landscapes, altered economic laws, perplexing tax laws and procedures, false cultural theories and intricate regulation. Therefore, to get into a business market, managers of a company that engages in international business must examine the subsequent components of the global business environment.

Evaluating the Global Business Environment

Waves of reform, globalisation and privatisation have impacted the global commerce environment so drastically that manufacturers, importers and legislators in developing nations like India have struggled to react to arising developments and obstacles, particularly troubling the constantly changing trade system, as displayed by both opposing globalisation and internationalisation discussions. Some of the main developments and obstacles are as follows:

- WTO contracts, for instance, seek to update the trade system and boost foreign trade operations on the global market. On the contrary, the United States protectionist policies, combined with the United Kingdom's Brexit, demonstrate the difficulties a global marketer faces in capturing global trade possibilities.
- The proliferation of different trade pacts and the constantly developing non-tariff system, particularly the Toilets and Phytosanitary and Scientific Measurements, have created novel difficulties for globally participating companies in terms of standard adherence.
- The technical development under Industry 4.0 has driven companies to alter their production procedures, company viewpoints and advertising approaches to meet the requirements of their clients.
- The worldwide epidemic has thrown a wrench in the global supply chain. The latest sourcing approach adopted by large retailers is the 'China Plus One approach', which means that large sellers are reorganising their supply chain outside China, providing possibilities for growth to nations in the Southeast Asia area.
- There is a rekindled emphasis on substituting essential imports, which has resulted in the implementation of multiple initiatives aimed at improving local production. 'Independent India' and 'Production-related Rewards' are examples of this in India.
- Numerous countries are in major debt trouble, such as Pakistan, Sri Lanka and Turkey; nearly all African and Central American nations, and so on. They are looking for economic help from the IMF and additional growth organisations.

- Politically, the globe is becoming increasingly hazardous. The Individual Republic of China's aggression, both economic and political, is a source of worry for the globe. China's debt-trap regulations are weakening the global economy.

To thrive in global markets, any company has to evaluate and determine its competitive edge in the context of the global business environment. Indian companies, big and small, ought to refocus on working on how successfully such aspects of their competitive edge may be linked with essential marketplace characteristics.

Political Environment

A nation's political environment affects business and company operations. Numerous businesses in nations such as the United States are accustomed to a calm operating environment; nevertheless, this might be uncommon in other nations. Because economics and politics are intertwined, a nation's political environment has an impact on how businesses operate both locally and internationally.

Concepts, hypotheses and positions are referred to as political ideologies. Understanding how these ideas and hypotheses can be applied or used to further business objectives is crucial. Multiple political ideologies can coexist in one nation (like India). A political structure can withstand a variety of often opposing political ideologies because each one will have a pressure category that works to balance it out.

Different Political Ideologies' Effects on a Nation's Limits

Political ideologies diverge, because of disparities in geographical location, polity, history, language, faith, culture and defense of national borders. When a political structure breaks down, larger countries or areas divide into smaller entities (*e.g.*, USSR). Now that, we have a better understanding of the political landscape, let's talk about the different types of government structure. These are listed in the following order:

- *Pluralism*: It is a philosophy of politics that is predicated on the idea that individuals with various origins, views and lives may coexist in an identical society. In addition, everyone has an equal opportunity to engage in politics and engage with the procedure of making decisions that benefit the society. It is about having political systems that embrace and incorporate minority categories based on their gender, position, culture or religion. Scandinavian nations serve as models of pluralism.

- *Totalitarianism*: A political structure at its most severe, totalitarianism is characterised by a single authoritarian political party. Furthermore, the political structure undermines civil liberties, the free press, and the ability to arrange by outlawing every opposition group, outlawing individual liberties, and placing the state's power over everyone. The public is subject to intense control by the system, which governs their private and public lives. China and North Korea, for instance, are leading instances of totalitarian rule and authoritarianism in the most severe and comprehensive forms.
- *Democracy*: Global companies favour democratic nations as the location of their corporate affairs. The main explanation for this is that democratic standards typically guarantee freedom, particularly financial liberty and legal privileges that protect the interests of both private citizens and corporate entities.

Political Structure's Effect on Administration Decision-Making

Being an aspect of a distinct political structure exposes any company operating in the global market to various political risks. Political risk arises when a nation's political environment makes it difficult for foreign businesses to conduct business there.

- *Political Hazard Factors and Categories*: Numerous forms of political risk can impede a business's ability to operate, such as governmental seizure of property, recurrent strikes and lockouts that impair the productivity of the business. Issues like the Russia-Ukraine conflict in 2022 can result from profound shifts in the political ideologies of a nation's leadership, which can cause civil unrest and the disintegration of ties between the governments of the residents and host countries.

- *Micro and Macropolitical Hazards*: Micropolitical hazards arise from political acts directed toward a specific foreign expenditure business. For example, following the 2020 armed forces conflict in Ladakh, India, banned foreign expenditures from nations with whom it shares boundaries without the consent of their governments, mainly to prevent hostile expenditures from China. On the other hand, they are seen as macropolitical hazards, if they are directed towards a sizeable portion of foreign shareholders.

There are two types of governance economic intervention: 'distinctive intervention' or minimal interference and 'communal intervention' or highest disruption. Businesses typically favour centrally managed bureaucracy led by a reliable political party. A US company that relocates from its distinctive home nation to a communal host nation like South Korea, Germany or Turkey will need to create new plans for all its partners, including the administration, vendors, consumers and rivals.

Economic Environment

The economic growth of the 193 nations that make up the world varies greatly. One of the most important decisions a Multi-national Company (MNC) must make is where in these nations to establish its presence and grow. An MNC would be guided by two primary variables: first, the simplicity of access to manufacturing variables (labour, raw materials, etc.) and second, the circumstances of demand (the marketplace dimensions, rate of expansion, etc.). Comprehending the dynamics of global country classification systems is crucial for comprehending the economic landscape.

Classification Based on Revenue

The nations are often categorised according to their gross domestic product (GDP) or gross national product (GNP) per capita. The GNP is the sum of all final products and services generated by a country each year plus the revenue of its citizens such as those who live overseas. Revenue from non-residents residing in a specific nation is excluded. GDP considers the entire amount of financial action that occurs within the boundaries of a nation, irrespective of whether it is the outcome of local or foreign expenditure. The amount of financial action per citizen of a nation in a year is known as gross national income (GNI) per capita.

Classification Based on Area

Multi-national Corporations (MNCs) find significance in the different areas and their categorizations. To design and framework their businesses and to market their goods, MNCs examine these marketplaces along geographical lines. Geographical areas are also taken into consideration when planning the logistics activities. The growth phase of these economies is also reflected in specific areas.

Classification Based on Economic Structure

An economic framework is a manufacturing, dispersion and usage structure that falls somewhere between 'unconstrained' and 'repressed'.

Classification Depending on Economy Types

There are four distinct kinds of economies.

1. A market system is one in which the private industry owns and controls economic assets. They are controlled by private businesses rather than the administration or public industry, as in the United States of America and the United Kingdom.
2. Command Economy—the administration or the public sector owns and controls the financial assets. The central administration of a nation depending on the Central Planning regulates the manufacturing and handling of products as well as the provision of assistance, as in China and the USSR before its breakdown into Russia, among other nations.
3. Conventional Economy—in this case, financial choices depend on centuries-old traditions and convictions passed

down through centuries, as in numerous African nations, particularly tribal areas.

4. Mixed Economy—numerous nations in the Mixed Economic System have a combination of all the three kinds of economies mentioned earlier. For instance, France and India have features of public and private industry ownership and management.

Technological Environment

Technology is among the most significant influences on contemporary companies. Two aspects of technology stand out. The first is quicker interaction and the subsequent one is lower technology costs. Let us initially address communication velocity; you will find that the expense of communicating has become just a small percentage of what it was a decade or two ago. Furthermore, the environment for communication has undergone an entire shift with the arrival of more recent and more intelligent instruments, such as e-mail, WhatsApp, Zoom Call and Google Meet, as well as the opening of different programs, such as MS Teams and Webex. The advancement of Internet-related technologies has allowed the development of effortless and affordable communication all over the globe.

The number of web users across the globe is nearly doubling every three to five years. The distribution of consumers of the Internet has the greatest entry registered by North America and the smallest by African nations. India has the third biggest population of online users in terms of absolute numbers just behind China and the USA, yet when it comes to access to the Internet, it is just 64% in India as contrasted with 95% in the US and 83% in China.

The world economy is seeing a production shift with novel inventions in technology like 3D Printing and Publishing, Artificial Intelligence, Bar-coded/Automatic recognition, Big Data, Blockchain, Cloud Computing, Computer-aided Design (CAD), Embedded Devices, Business Resource preparation, Internet-of-Things (IoT), Radio Frequency & Identification (RFID), Automation, Sensor Networking, Wireless Communication, and so on. These innovations are changing the upstream, horizontal and downward supply chains of companies. A company uses technologies to win over consumers in competitive marketplaces.

Regular technological advancements cause adjustments to be made to international firms' strategic business plans. Even though access and initial expenses for businesses are prohibitive, organisations still need to establish a dominant place in the market. To gain traction in foreign markets, businesses are forming collaborative ventures and looking for ways to combine their advantages and abilities. The impact of evolving electronic communications and technical advancements on global business is immense; however, continuous innovation is imperative to maintain a sustainable competitive edge.

Thus, technology has the potential to be both 'beneficial and destructive'. The goal of technological advancements must be to innovate and bring about shifts that raise the standard of living for all people while also improving the standard of goods and client service.

Ecological Environment

Environmental problems are gaining global prominence. Several environmental alterations are being brought about by unsustainable manufacturing practices, expanding requirements for development and an ever-growing global population. Irresponsible industrial development, deforestation, traffic jams, growing populations, systemic failure in the civic organisation and illiteracy constitute the main causes of environmental degradation.

The loss of the ozone layer results from the manufacture of industrial products like air conditioning units and refrigerators, which release harmful gases called Chlorofluorocarbons (CFCs). Climate and weather shifts are the results of this. Industry-related waste releases have contaminated the air, water and soil. Numerous commercial establishments currently employ efficient methods for managing waste and treating wastewater. Corporate entities and family-owned enterprises no longer have the exclusive right to make business decisions. A variety of key players, including executives, staff members, vendors, distributors, customers and government representatives, have a say in how businesses plan for the adverse environmental impacts of both suggested and existing sectors. Consequently, there is a perception that businesses ought to exhibit social responsibility. To protect the environment, businesses have created guidelines and procedures. They are made to incorporate provisions related to minimising ecological problems, into their business plans.

Social and Cultural Environment

Managers must understand the cultures of other nations in the modern global environment. This is a crucial matter and disregarding cultural sensitivity could have disastrous results that could even put commercial transactions in jeopardy. Before embarking on a project abroad, executives ought to complete their research by familiarizing themselves with vital aspects of foreign cultures. This could be accomplished by taking a brief program in a foreign language, receiving cross-cultural training, and becoming familiar with business manners and procedures. Through cultural direction, one can accomplish this and prevent errors.

Cultural Recognition and Dynamics

A manager can gain an understanding of the dynamics of diverse cultures through specific methods that are as follows:

1. The nation serves as a frame of reference for cultural disparities that typically arise from disparate cultures, customs, opinions, principles and faiths. To comprehend and value cultural distinctions, it is therefore imperative to contrast variations in national cultures.
2. *Dynamics and Cultural Creation*: Children pick up cultural traits from their elders at a young age. Value structures and culture are passed down from one generation to the next as well. Cultural shifts occur as time passes for several causes, including increased contact with foreign cultures, moving to a different location, making friends with individuals from different cultures, foreign media, and so on. Cultural imperialism is the term used to describe when the culture

of a nation is altered, because of a foreign nation's culture being forcibly imposed upon it.

3. *Language Fostering Cultural Stability*: Spoken languages like French, English, and so on may be used to identify a culture. Individuals, who speak comparable tongues in a community are probably also of comparable cultural origins. Since distinct languages are utilised inside the boundaries of numerous nations, these nations have distinct cultures.
4. *Religion Fostering Cultural Stability*: A nation's company procedures are influenced by its culture, which is reflected in the religion its citizens follow. The culture of a nation is influenced by a variety of factors, including weekends, work schedules, dietary preferences, religious beliefs and ways of existence.
5. *Culturally-oriented Social Behaviours*: Given how these practices affect businesses operating in foreign markets, executives need to be conscious of them.

Social Stratification

Different cultural norms may be employed to create social strata in a society. An individual's birth, success, political affiliation, faith or other characteristics can all be taken into consideration, when ranking them. Social stratification may have an impact on intended marketplace selection, HR policies and procedures, and other related decisions.

The subsequent cultural traits affect an individual's societal standing:

1. *Merit as the foundation for choice*: In numerous developed nations, competency or merit serves as the foundation for hiring decisions or job promotions. Because each worker has the chance to be compared based on their performance, this fosters positive rivalry in the workplace. Because expertise matters in managerial capacities, seniority has more influence over decisions about promotions in Japan. It can occasionally result in less performance competitiveness and even discord among junior staff members.
2. *Groups according to Gender*: Social perceptions and orientations toward men and women in society vary

among nations. We can use the Political Risk Insurance (PRI) instance of the Middle East and other nations with a large proportion of Muslims in this respect. Islamic legislation outlines distinct perspectives and principles concerning women's roles within society. For example, the Islamic clergy forbids women from going to school, holding office jobs or even employment in certain countries like Saudi Arabia, Afghanistan and Sudan. As far as Saudi Arabia is concerned, items have been gradually and partly altering lately.

3. *Age-based Teams*: Age is a common indicator of expertise and knowledge in numerous nations. The workforce's superannuation is set at age sixty or sixty-five. Because, they need young, energetic workers, numerous businesses set the age for working at a younger age to favour younger workers.
4. *Family-based Groups*: In certain societies, a family's societal standing decides a member's place in the company rather than an individual's accomplishments. In recent times, family-owned companies have become increasingly significant, as non-family members encounter challenges, when attempting to advance up the management chain.
5. *Source of Living*: Individuals choose a career or way of income based on the societal and financial status associated with vocations. Teachers are viewed as more important than executives in certain nations. In contrast, individuals in other societies choose to pursue careers in medicine or engineering due to the high status associated with these fields of study.

Coping Mechanisms for Cultural Variations

Given the diversity of cultures across nations, executives must create suitable approaches to address these disparities.

1. *Adapting Slightly or Not at All*: Executives of a company with global operations must adapt to employees from different cultural backgrounds. However, certain cultures that grant foreigners greater autonomy than their citizens need less acclimatization. Cultural resemblance between

regions can also be present; Argentina and Uruguay are two examples of such resemblance. If the company expands and diversifies to such similar nations, the staff members in those nations will readily adapt to a new culture.

2. *Communication*: Good communication is the key to overcoming cultural disparities. In addition to written and spoken forms, communication also involves sign language.
3. *Oral and Written Language*: Linguistic distinctions cause communication issues between nations. Determining the precise meaning and significance of phrases in two distinct tongues can be challenging. For instance, the United States and the United Kingdom use various spellings, pronunciations and implications for more than 4,000 English phrases.
4. *Silent Language*: This category includes non-verbal signals, such as kinesis and closeness (body motion), gestures, positions, hap-ties (contact), paralanguage (feelings) and preferred colours. Misunderstood body language, such as standing too near or too far away, or silent communication can sabotage a crucial business transaction.
5. *Cultural Shock*: A worker must adjust to novel cultural signals and language, when they relocate from their home nation to a new one. As a result, businesses arrange for cultural training courses for staff members leaving for their overseas assignments. Workers, who have finished a foreign assignment may also experience opposite cultural adjustment upon returning to residence.

Case Study: Copying Mechanisms to Navigate Cultural Variances

Japan is now home to Zenith International, a worldwide software development firm with its headquarters located in the United States. The organization wanted to create a diversified and creative work environment while making use of the high- level of expertise possessed by software engineers in Japan. There were major cultural differences between the American and Japanese offices. The US team promoted free communication among staff members and gave them room to express their ideas and take initiative. The Japanese team, on the other hand, was used to a hierarchical organization that respected authority and relied on group decision-making. Due to these cultural differences, there were miscommunications: the Japanese team thought the American approach was excessively combative, while the American team thought their Japanese counterparts were overly docile.

Coping Mechanism Implementation

a. *Cross-cultural Training Seminars*: Staff members from both offices attended seminars hosted by Zenith International. The teams learned about one another's work ethics, communication preferences and cultural conventions through these sessions.

b. *Mentor-mentee Program*: They started a program wherein employees from various departments are paired with mentors. Through one-on-one conversations, this program assisted team members in appreciating and comprehending one another's cultural viewpoints.

c. *Flexible Communication Channels*: To accommodate different comfort levels in expressing thoughts, the company created a variety of communication channels, including formal and informal ones.

d. *Frequent Team-building Exercises*: To foster camaraderie among team members, they planned both in-person and virtual team-building exercises.

e. *Feedback Mechanism*: An anonymous feedback mechanism was set-up so that staff members could voice any issues or recommendations. These were then discussed in team meetings.

Outcomes

The groups started to recognize and capitalize on their cultural differences, which resulted in more creative problem-solving and efficient co-operation. As a result of the staff members' growing awareness of one another's working methods and cultural backgrounds, the workplace became more polite and united. The team's ability to solve problems was improved by exposure to a variety of viewpoints, which was advantageous for complicated projects. Teams were more prepared to deal with miscommunications when they did arise, and their frequency had dropped dramatically.

In summary, the global business environment represents a dynamic and interconnected web of external forces that significantly impact a company's operations on the international stage. Navigating this complex landscape involves grappling with political, economic, technological, ecological and socio-cultural factors. The intricate interplay of these elements shapes the dynamics of global business, influencing decision-making and strategies. Cultivating a deep understanding of cultural nuances becomes crucial, necessitating adaptive approaches, effective communication and coping mechanisms to bridge diverse perspectives. As companies face difficulties and opportunities emerging from political ideologies, economic frameworks, technological advancements, environmental considerations and social stratification, their success relies on strategic insight and flexibility. In an era of rapid global evolution, businesses must not only navigate external variables but also leverage technological advancements responsibly for sustainable growth. The ability to innovate and thrive within this ever-shifting global context rests on the resilience and strategic foresight of organisations.

Activity

1. What role does proficient communication play in enhancing a company's performance in global markets?
2. Explore the ways in which communication strategies for businesses in international markets are shaped by waves of reform, globalization and privatization.
3. Explore the ways in which executives can utilise effective communication strategies to manoeuvre through politically uncertain environments.
4. How can companies tailor their communication to address economic variations in different regions?
5. Examine the effects of technology on communication in the realm of global business, highlighting the role of tools, such as e-mail, video-conferencing and collaborative platforms.

6. Examine how global business interactions strike a balance between leveraging technology for communication and preserving a human touch.
7. Discuss how effective communication contributes to the integration of environmental considerations into business plans.
8. Discuss the potential effects of communication errors in social and cultural settings.
9. Explore communication strategies for effectively overseeing global teams characterised by diverse cultural backgrounds.

Part II
Cultural Intelligence in Business

3
Understanding Cultural Diversity

Culture

Cultural definitions encompass a broad spectrum of viewpoints. The following are some of the terms and phrases that individuals in the company training sessions employ to characterise culture: nourishment, faith, dialect, music, area or geographical location, race, clothes, and so on. Usually, someone raises their hand hesitantly and states, 'I believe culture encompasses more than just that'. It's the things, we choose not to notice, such as our gender-related views and opinions. Both are true: culture is a representation of both the tangible and intangible matters that are visible to us.

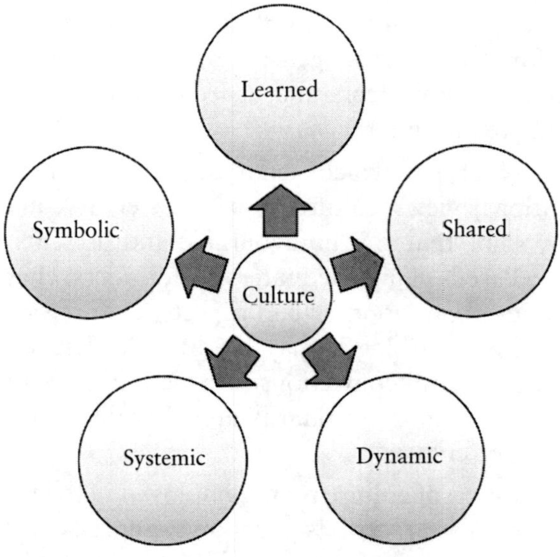

Figure 3.1: Elements of Culture

Source: https://saylordotorg.github.io/text_leading-with-cultural-intelligence/s04-02-what-is-culture.html

The iceberg, a metaphor for culture that is frequently employed, is a fantastic way to show both the physical and the ethereal. The 'point of the iceberg', which is thought to make up ten per cent of the object, is what most individuals concentrate on when discussing culture. Ninety per cent of the iceberg is beneath the surface of the water. When dealing with cross-cultural circumstances, most executives focus on what they observe—the point of the iceberg. This implies that the underlying cultural tensions and problems are never addressed. Solutions end up being transient stitches applied over long-established cultural structures.

A leader once defined and described culture as 'a monster'. He elaborated on his remarks following which the group laughed a little bit: 'It's so chaotic and on occasion, it's too much to handle'. It's frightening as well since you have no idea what you're getting into. For a lot of individuals and companies that operate in multicultural environments, what he said is accurate. Cleaning up cultural blunders, miscommunications and disruptions is undoubtedly unpleasant, and if left unattended, can lead to significant cultural disputes. One of the skills required for cultural intelligence work is the capacity to own up to one's cultural errors and a dedication to understanding the benefits of culture.

This definition, which examines culture in all of its manifestations, views culture as a monster. It could even be argued by some that it is unfavourable and presents culture in a bad way. Based on my encounters with leaders, characterizing culture is not about good or bad aspects; culture simply exists, which is why describing it may be difficult. The statement of group principles and convictions, instruction in groups and the manifestation of those standards are typically included in the descriptions of culture.

A description of culture that is employed in the material and will help you in your work is as follows: Edgar Schein provided the original definition of culture, which has been adopted here.

A collection of individuals, who educate each other that their mind-sets, actions and viewpoints are the correct methods to behave, think and feel are known as a culture. It is made up of their common beliefs, values and presumptions.

You may find it useful to approach culture in the following five methods:

- Culture is learned.
- Culture is shared.
- Culture is dynamic.
- Culture is systemic.
- Culture is symbolic.

Concept of Diversity

Respect and acceptance are two aspects of the notion of diversity. It entails realizing how distinctive each person is and appreciating the distinctions. These distinctions may pertain to aspects like ethnicity, age, social standing, physical capabilities, religious convictions, and so on. Therefore, it's important to investigate these disparities in a supportive, encouraging and safe-setting.

The employment population of today is made up of individuals, who are diverse and, who share a range of views, needs, desires, values and work behaviours. It is also more varied in terms of race, ethnic background, gender and national background. For a company to succeed, executives must be aware of the diversity that the staff members bring with them in addition to the cultural heritage from which they originate. Because of this, executives in both public and private companies must comprehend, anticipate and handle the fascinating nature of workforce diversity. Diversity is a crucial idea that requires close examination. According to research conducted by Builtin (it is the online community for start-ups and tech companies), diverse companies enjoy 2.5 times higher cash flow per employee than their peers and diverse management teams have increased business revenue by 19%.

Diversity administration was initially highlighted by R. Roosevelt, Thomas (1990). Diversity presents a wide range of challenges for businesses, which is why it must be managed cautiously.

There are several definitions of diversity or workforce diversity offered by various writers. Among them are the following:

- According to Van Knippenberg and Schippers (2007), diversity is a feature of a social system (*i.e.*, category, company and society) that indicates the extent to which the participants of the group vary from one another in either an objective or subjective way, without assuming that all participants of the category are conscious of these distinctions or that subjective distinction have a significant connection with objective distinctions.
- Workforce diversity, according to Carrell (2006), is the variety of individuals within a company that can impact an assignment or connection. These differences include gender, race, age, religious beliefs and culture. It involves investigating these distinctions in a secure, encouraging and supportive setting. It is about gaining mutual comprehension and going outside basic acceptance to embrace and celebrate the many facets of diversity that each member of the company possesses.
- According to B.Y. Kim (2006), diversity may be defined as the wide range of differences that set the staff of a company apart. This multifaceted perspective on diversity is predicated on the idea that there are countless ways in which people may vary from each other. Certain dimensions—like race and gender—are more obvious than others, like values, character, training, expertise, gender identity and religion.
- Workforce diversity is defined by Soni and Vidu (2000) as the variations in individuals depending on race or ethnic background, religious belief, physical or mental impairment, sexual identity and financial standing.
- Diversity is described as "the existence of staff members from different cultural and social backgrounds inside a business" by Wentling and Palma Rivas (2000). Cultural characteristics including colour, gender, age, physical ability, ethnicity and race are all included in diversity.

Age, national origin, faith, impairment, gender identity, values, ethnic backgrounds, schooling, language, way of living, opinions, physical characteristics and socio-economic standing are some examples of the wider definition of diversity.

Cultural Diversity

A profitable company must embrace cultural diversity as a fundamental component of its daily operations and have an unwavering dedication to this goal. The following are the opinions of various writers regarding cultural diversity:

- According to Ivancevich and Gilbert (2000) as well as Nkomo and Cox (1996), the definition of cultural diversity is situational and particular. Cultural diversity is widely regarded by modern researchers as a significant characteristic that sets one person apart from another, encompassing both overt and covert traits.
- According to Doherty and Chelladurai (1999), cultural diversity refers to the distinct sets of principles, opinions, mind-sets and standards that people have due to having certain shared traits with others, and also symbolic language, customs and behaviours.
- Cultural diversity is defined by Cox (1994) as identity formed by affiliation in categories that are socio-culturally unique meaning that they share standards, principles or customs that are separate from those of other teams. This identity can include race, ethnic background, nationality, faith, sexual orientation and other aspects of distinction.

Drawing from the previously stated descriptions, the subsequent characteristics of cultural diversity can be identified:

Cultural Diversity Features

- Cultural diversity has two sides: when managed well, it may serve as a competitive benefit; when mishandled, it can lead to disagreements and discontent within a company.

- Cultural diversity transcends the notions of equal chances and positive actions.
- Cultural diversity encompasses not just the primary aspects, which are sexual orientation, age, race and ethnicity, but also the supplementary aspects, which are personality traits, faith and education.
- Maintaining cultural diversity is a continuous process that must be carried out in response to the shifting requirements of the diverse workforce. It is not a one-time event.

In summary, cultural diversity encompasses both visible and invisible elements that contribute to individual distinctions, such as sexual orientation, faith, physical impairment, family history, racial or ethnic background, and hierarchical position, as well as language, education, occupation and ways of life.

Despite having the same significance, the terms diversity, workforce diversity and cultural diversity were employed interchangeably in this research.

Cultural Diversity Significance

Modern businesses now recognise the value of hiring, developing and advancing a diverse workforce. The connection between individuals from diverse cultural backgrounds and the company is now acknowledged by the human resources administration method. The fundamental tenets of this strategy can be derived from Bolman and Deal's (2003) findings:

- Individuals and groups depend on one another. Organisations are present to satisfy human requirements.
- Either or both of them will be harmed when there is an insufficient match between the person and the company.
- Both parties benefit, when there is a strong fit between the person and the company.

As a result, cultural diversity is no longer so much a requirement as a need. A supportive setting is produced when executives recognise the cultural norms and principles of their staff. By doing this, the business can successfully foster an environment of confidence and collaboration.

Cultural Diversity Difficulties in Indian Business

Opportunities and difficulties coexist side by side. The business must overcome obstacles if it hopes to reap the benefits of cultural diversity. Among the main obstacles is:

- *Communication*: To ensure the achievement of diversity initiatives, the business must conquer the persistent cultural and language obstacles that lead to poor communication, an absence of co-operation, and so on.
- *Resilience to Transformation*: Workers typically oppose change, because it takes a period to comprehend and accept changes. The workers must get rid of the mind-set that says, 'I am employed to accomplish it in this manner', before they can embrace the transformation.
- *Diversity at work execution*: Companies must, at all costs, put their diversity regulations into practice. It should go without saying that initially, staff members may not concur or like identical things. However, this is referred to as a difficulty.
- The execution of regulations promoting diversity in jobs presents an enormous hurdle for all supports and boosters of diversity. It is not enough to merely mandate staff members complete diversity training; instead, diversity must be internalised, that is, it must become an integral part of all organisational processes and policies.

Cultural Diversity Opportunities

Managing diversity gives any company a competitive edge, which boosts earnings. A business can reap the following rewards or benefits that are culturally diverse:

1. *Improved client support*: Given that the majority of businesses have a varied clientele, a diverse workforce is better able to comprehend and interact with a wider range of clients, meeting their varied requirements in the process.
2. *Improved problem-solving*: In contrast to a group made up of individuals of the same kind, a diverse team offers the

business access to more data, a wider range of thoughts and opinions, and more methods of problem-solving. To put it succinctly, diversity can provide a deeper understanding for addressing difficulties.

3. *Greater tolerance for differing viewpoints*: A diverse workforce encompasses a wide range of ideas that represent various points of view and moral principles. To take full advantage of these diverse viewpoints, businesses need to embrace staff members, who have differing opinions.
4. *Greater flexibility*: A company needs to be capable of reacting fast to competitive behaviour and swiftly altering client demands.
5. *Appreciating equality among and input from people*: To fully realise the value coming from the benefits of more data and broader, richer viewpoints, the business must foster an atmosphere where people feel that their efforts are valued and that they work in an equitable setting.
6. *More creative*: Possessing a diverse workforce helps a business, because it allows individuals with various experiences to view the same issue from various perspectives, which leads to more creative and original problem-solving and decision-making.
7. *Improves the corporate image*: Companies are worried about their reputation in the community, or what people believe about them, and the emotions that they associate with them when their names are stated. A favourable public perception aids in the business's capacity to draw in clients, workers and shareholders. Having a positive reputation as a business that embraces diversity can work wonders for the corporate image.

Cultural Diversity Management Procedures

The phases involved in the strategic procedure of diversity management are as follows:

1. *Evaluation*: Through an examination of the reasons and effects of the difficulties, each business must determine its present policy, statistical and cultural status.

2. *Establishing goals*: The next phase involves establishing goals, which usually involves components like description of the business's ideal post-diversity management state, the business instance for preventing prejudice and the dedication of upper management. All these components play an integral role in ensuring successful outcomes.
3. *Raising consciousness*: Raising consciousness is necessary at this crucial stage. Diverse workers at all phases, particularly executives, need to have their understanding of diversity promoted.
4. *Policy growth*: All staff members are involved in the implementation of the novel systems. These ought not to be mandated.
5. *Controlling the change*: This calls for a range of educational programs. These may involve initiatives created especially to help under-represented categories comprehend the organisational culture and gain the necessary abilities. It is necessary to create particular diversity management procedures and initiatives, with an emphasis on instruction, evaluation and selection. Training classes should also be provided to raise consciousness, recognise cultural diversity and handle various cultural contexts.
6. *To maintain momentum*: This calls for the participation of an upper management professional—who need not be from the HR department—who can carry on the procedure in tandem with the labour organisation.
7. To evaluate the accomplishments of diversity management procedures in terms of business advantages like enhanced relationships with clients, improved efficiency and higher revenue. This is the final phase in the process.

Approaches to Handle Cultural Diversity

Three approaches have been recognised by Adler (1997) to handle cultural diversity within the organisation.

1. *Disregard cultural disparities*: The executives in the company that use this strategy are unaware of how cultural disparities affect the company. Local businesses are the ones that use

this tactic the most. Managers and staff in these kinds of businesses think that their method of management and organisation is the only one. They consider diversity to be merely a meaningless idea. Therefore, there is no place for initiatives aimed at managing diversity effectively, reducing the detrimental effects of cultural disparities or enhancing the benefits of diversity.

2. *Reduce cultural disparities*: Ethnocentric businesses primarily use this tactic. Here, executives are aware of the diversity of cultures, but just as a cause of issues. In an ethnocentric business, executives take the stance that organising and managing 'our manner is the most effective way'. They consider other people's methods of operation to be sub-par. Executives think that the best way to lessen diversity is to lessen the issues caused by distinctions. The advantages of diversity are not taken into account. For this reason, a company like this would rather have a homogeneous workforce. Therefore, by limiting the potential for having a culturally diverse workforce within the business, ethnocentric businesses continue to be deprived of or unaffected by the advantages of getting a diverse workforce.

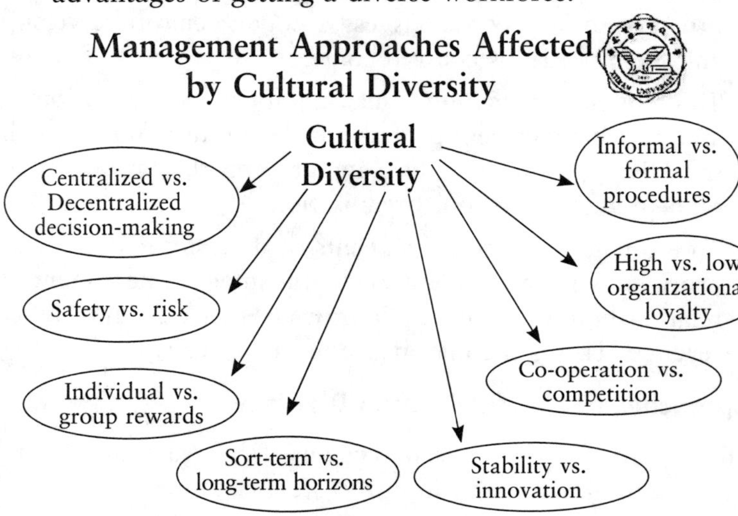

Figure 3.2: Management Approaches Impacted by Cultural Diversity

Source: https://www.slideshare.net/MingLi1/cross-cultural-management-14532203

3. *Handle cultural variations*: Synergistic businesses are those that employ an approach to handle distinctions. These kinds of businesses understand how cultural diversity has both positive and negative impacts. These executives feel that although there are differences between our strategy and theirs in terms of behaviour and management, neither is the most effective manner to organise and handle. Businesses that are synergistic effectively handle cultural diversity by providing executives and employees with the necessary training to identify and capitalise on cultural disparities.

Cultural Relativism

Cultural relativism asserts that the values, beliefs and customs of a culture ought to be understood in the context specific to that culture. It underscores the absence of universal benchmarks for appraising all cultures, advocating instead for the evaluation of each culture according to its distinct attributes. This perspective urges individuals to withhold judgment and approach cultural practices with an open mind, acknowledging the manifold diversity of human experiences.

Cultural diversity, cultural relativism and international business communication are intricately linked within the global business landscape. Cultural diversity encompasses the assortment of cultural backgrounds existing in international business environments. Acknowledging and valuing this diversity is imperative for successful communication. Business professionals must comprehend how cultural differences influence communication styles, decision-making processes and business etiquette. Cultural relativism is particularly pertinent in international business communication, as it discourages ethnocentrism—the inclination to assess other cultures based on one's own cultural norms. Embracing a culturally relative perspective allows business professionals to navigate communication challenges without imposing their own cultural biases.

Cultural relativism promotes the importance of being culturally sensitive in business communication. It highlights the value of comprehending and respecting a variety of cultural practices, thereby encouraging more efficient and respectful interactions in international business settings.

Recognizing the interconnected nature of these concepts suggests that strategies in international business communication should be flexible to various dimensions of diversity, encompassing not only cultural differences but also factors, such as gender, ethnicity and socio-economic backgrounds.

Recognizing cultural diversity and incorporating cultural relativism into communication play a role in fostering inclusive practices. Inclusivity is crucial for cultivating positive relationships with international partners, clients and employees. Successful negotiations and relationship building in international business depend on effective communication. The comprehension of cultural diversity and the adoption of a culturally relative approach improve the capability to navigate complex business scenarios.

To sum up, the intricate nature of cultural definitions highlights the diverse range of perspectives present in the global business setting. The iceberg analogy effectively encapsulates both the visible and unseen facets of culture, stressing the importance of addressing underlying cultural tensions for lasting solutions. Describing culture as a monster, as articulated by a leader, acknowledges its intricate and challenging nature. Edgar Schein's definition offers a comprehensive insight, emphasizing that culture is acquired, shared, dynamic, systemic and symbolic. Diversity, whether manifested in the workforce or cultural landscape, requires acknowledgment, acceptance and proactive management. The value of diversity is not merely a prerequisite but a crucial element in cultivating a supportive and co-operative environment. Despite challenges in managing cultural diversity, the advantages, such as enhanced client support, inventive problem-solving and a positive corporate image, position it as a strategic necessity. Cultural relativism reinforces the importance of culturally aware communication in the global business realm. Understanding the interplay among cultural diversity, cultural relativism and international business communication underscores the significance of inclusive approaches for successful engagements in our diverse world.

Embracing these principles enhances the ability to navigate complexities, promoting positive relationships and successful outcomes in the global business arena.

Activity

1. Elaborate on the metaphorical concept of culture as an iceberg and its importance in comprehending both the apparent and concealed elements of a culture.
2. Examine the leader's analogy describing culture as a 'monster' and identify the aspects of culture that make it appear disorderly and challenging to navigate.
3. What makes it vital for businesses to examine and acknowledge the diverse perspectives that individuals bring to the workplace?
4. How can a diverse workforce contribute to a company's overall success and competitive advantage?
5. Define cultural relativism and discuss how it promotes a nuanced comprehension of cultural practices.
6. Give examples of how employing a culturally relative approach can prevent miscommunication and misunderstandings.
7. How can business professionals embed inclusive practices within their communication strategies?
8. Suggest approaches for businesses to effectively navigate the intricacies of cultural diversity in international communication.

4

Cultural Intelligence: Key Concepts and Importance

Introduction

Cultural intelligence (CQ) is described as a person's capacity to operate efficiently in culturally varied settings. This overall capacity or ability is made up of four interconnected features: CQ motivates or inspires CQ (*i.e.*, the capacity to control and endure power and also trust in adapting to cross-cultural circumstances), CQ understanding or mental CQ (*i.e.*, awareness and comprehension of cultures, such as resemblance and distinctions), and CQ approach or meta-cognitive CQ (such as the capacity to organise, stay conscious and track mental procedures). These skills importantly complement one another to promote behavioural adaptability in multicultural environments. CQ applies to various cultures and sub-cultures, assisting people and businesses in improving work function in extremely varied and/or worldwide business contexts.

CQ is a malleable competency that may be enhanced through instruction and guidance, in conjunction with self-evaluations and plans for personal growth (in a manner that enhances the impact of all of these actions). Furthermore, after participating in a CQ training course, people and groups are better prepared to advance their intercultural skills through job duties (*e.g.*, functioning in a multicultural environment, completing a global project, or interacting in international bargaining and opening up fresh markets or broaden revenue to vital global clients).

CQ Origins

The concept of CQ has been developed, encouraged and moulded by several key people. Emotional intelligence (EQ) also contributed significantly to the concept of a multifaceted structure for intelligence, as opposed to a different structure based on 'g' or general intelligence. Although there is no question that people have broad intelligence and problem-solving abilities, there is sufficient evidence to add particularity to this concept by suggesting different 'classes' of intelligence or aspects.

Long before the emergence of CQ, the significance of adapting to other cultures was recognised. This simulation was created to assist people in comprehending the role culture serves in social relationships and to gain experience adapted to novel 'cultures' (although simulation cultures).

Any conversation about CQ should start with the concept of culture. Following all, culture is the heart of society, encompassing its systems and procedures. If culture evolved as a by-product of development to fight the danger of separation (and to assist in expressing adaptable characteristics of social relationships to protect the community) or as a response to mental requirements for meaning in the globe around us, it stays an essential component of how individuals communicate across geographical and societal borders.

The human urge to establish units and recognise oneself through definable subsets makes the development of culture unavoidable. It is obtained and conveyed primarily through representations such as their manifestations in artefacts. The fundamental basis of culture includes inherited and chosen concepts, as well as their associated values. Culture can be viewed as influencing the character of social systems as they evolve. Hofstede (1991) offers a widely cited description of culture. His standpoint is that culture can be best understood as an assortment of coding that individuals use inside a country or the software of the intellect. Communities build their groups and societal aggregation the regulations indicated by culture. Within a community, cross-generational transfer of cultural significance is inadequate; over the years, people gain shifts in cultural significance grasped by their predecessors that were poorly shared, so a couple of humans from a single culture might have slightly distinct interpretations for an identical incident or build, and these two people might have common significance with other parties within the community yet not with each other. While addressing ideas that are unique to specific cultures as opposed to those that are prevalent across cultures further difficulties develop.

Against the context of culture's complexities, CQ relates to a person's capacity to adjust and investigate different cultural settings by relying on three broad aspects: meta-cognition/cognition, drive and action. The mental processes/intellectual aspect relates to the data processing facets of intellect and can be understood by employing the component of self-concept. According to the self-concept hypothesis, the 'self' is a continuous interpretative framework that co-ordinates the majority of important intrapersonal and interpersonal activities. The mental processes/intellectual aspect of CQ may be defined as a person's overall understanding and wisdom retained in memory regarding cultural adjustment. Understanding oneself is not enough to achieve excellent CQ; consciousness does not ensure flexibility; versatility of self-concept and simplicity in incorporating novel aspects into it, on the other hand, are linked with elevated CQ, because comprehending novel cultures may necessitate giving up already present ideas of the reasons why individuals operate as they do.

CQ meta-cognition describes more advanced cognitive operations that occur as a component of an individual's processing of data or 'imagining about thinking'. Therefore, meta-cognition may be divided into two supplementary components: meta-cognitive understanding (what and the ways to handle understanding acquired in an array of contexts) and meta-cognitive encounter (what and the way to integrate pertinent events as a framework to subsequent conversations). The requirements put on learning about a novel culture that is minimal in prevalent with that of an expatriate executive, for instance, are high, and a person will probably understand that an enormous amount of focus and persistence is needed. The last component of meta-cognitive understanding is strategy factors, which are the processes employed to accomplish a specific objective.

Since much of what is needed in a new culture is piecing together trends into a coherent image—even if one is unsure of how this coherent image might look—meta-cognition is a crucial component of critical thinking. Higher levels of planning regarding people, locations and events are necessary to achieve this. This is the cause why a lot of cultural training courses fall short as they prioritise a particular instance over a broader meta-learning procedure. To train their international executives, numerous businesses give them data particular to each nation. This strategy is constrained not just by an individual's engagement with the training methodology, but also fails to sufficiently prepare an executive for comprehending and navigating new scenarios that are outside the purview of the training. To perform well, an elevated CQ individual needs to inductively construct an appropriate connection to the societal context. This necessitates a general yet comprehensive basis for understanding society and culture, akin to the instruction suggested by an anthropological perspective and encompassing subjects like societal connections, political and spiritual businesses, financial structures, and so on.

The second aspect of CQ is inspiration. Merely possessing knowledge about how a particular category of individuals might navigate the globe is insufficient. You must possess the ability and drive to apply this knowledge to generate a culturally relevant response. CQ guides and encourages adjustment to novel cultural contexts. A person's involvement, determination and self-worth are key components of inspiration. Since effective intercultural communication depends on an individual's belief in the effectiveness of societal discourse in a foreign cultural context, self-worth is crucial to CQ. After feeling early setbacks, an individual, who does not think they are capable of comprehending individuals from unfamiliar cultures tends to become disengaged. If CQ's inspiring component is lacking, modification won't happen.

The inspiring aspect of CQ is not fully described by effectiveness alone; deliberate and goal-oriented conduct is a significant and associated addition. Finding the objectives of people with diverse cultural and personal origins can be difficult in cross-cultural interactions. Numerous academics' works highlight the interplay between setting objectives and effectiveness standards. Emotions are produced during the assessment of the importance of information regarding our well-being. We only become emotionally reactive, when we acknowledge that we stand to acquire or lose a thing, that is, when the result of the deal matters to our objectives and happiness. As a result, objective evaluation is essential for both evoking the emotions that spur activity and for triggering a reaction toward accomplishing objectives. In other words, our objectives could serve as mental anchors, directing our conduct in the future.

Key Importance

Since Earley and Ang (2003) initially suggested the idea of cultural intelligence, a great deal of scientific investigation was done. Over the past 15 years, a significant area of research has focussed on the influence of cultural intelligence on specific results that are pertinent to working environments.

The capacity to function well in culturally diverse or globally immersive environments—such as when collaborating on an assignment with coworkers from different backgrounds or dealing with vendors or consumers in foreign markets—is one advantage of having an elevated CQ. This capacity for achievement extends to work environments with various forms of diversity (for instance, intergenerational or sexual diversity). Based on current research, it can be inferred that people and organisations possessing a significant CQ will enjoy several distinct advantages that have been characterised as psychological results (*e.g.*, successful cross-cultural adaptation, enhanced cultural assessment and elevated interpersonal confidence); behavioural results (for instance, enhanced decision-making, elevated degree of concept and sharing of data, innovative teamwork); and performance results (*e.g.*, successful cross-cultural bargaining; enhanced work output). Businesses can gain additional advantages in addition to the favourable effects of these personal and team-related results like higher revenue and money saved (from, say, implementing more creative approaches), increased global market growth, improved client assistance that is customised to meet the unique requirements of various client groups as well as improved HR strategies to draw and retain talent in the face of a more varied and international workforce. This part we will examine and go over the main advantages of CQ for people, groups, and companies in the parts that follow.

CQ and Cultural Knowledge

CQ and cultural knowledge share a dynamic and mutually reinforcing relationship, forming the bedrock of effective intercultural competence. Cultural knowledge serves as the cornerstone, encompassing a deep understanding of the social norms, traditions and values that define different cultures. This knowledge is not static; it evolves with exposure, experience and continuous learning, shaping individuals' ability to navigate and engage with diverse cultural landscapes.

Within the framework of CQ, cultural knowledge plays a pivotal role in the cognitive dimension. Individuals with high cognitive cultural intelligence possess a well-developed awareness and understanding of diverse cultural practices, allowing them to interpret and navigate cultural nuances effectively. This cognitive foundation facilitates the development of other CQ dimensions.

Cultural knowledge acts as a lens through which individuals can interpret and make sense of their own cultural biases and those of others, paving the way for more informed and culturally sensitive decision-making.

Furthermore, an enriched cultural knowledge contributes to increased adaptability and flexibility during cross-cultural engagements. As individuals deepen their comprehension of varied cultural norms and communication approaches, they gain improved skills to modify their conduct and communication methods to harmonise with the diverse expectations of cultural contexts. This flexibility stands out as an essential element of CQ empowering individuals not merely to operate proficiently in diverse environments, but also to cultivate substantial connections transcending cultural borders. In essence, the interplay between CQ and cultural knowledge underscores the crucial importance of having a well-grounded understanding of various cultures as a fundamental foundation for success in cross-cultural interactions.

Elevated Intercultural Adaptation

When it comes to emotionally and psychologically adjusting to new or different cultures (and sub-cultures), people with significant CQ do better. This makes it easier for people to operate across cultures and sub-cultures and reduces burnout while increasing resilience or the capacity for recovery under pressure. Culturally, intelligent people exhibit enhanced degrees of efficiency and endurance, and also bigger forbearance under pressure. Furthermore, people with excessive CQ find it easier to adapt to the uncertain, complicated and changing job requirements that are frequently present in cross-cultural settings (such as functioning in a multicultural group).

Case Study: Cultural Intelligence and Adaptation in a Global Company

Starbucks faced significant operational and cultural challenges, when it entered the Chinese market. Cultural awareness and adaptability helped the company prosper in a different industry. Starbucks entered the Chinese market in 1999 into a culture that was used to drinking tea and new to coffee as a leisure beverage. Another complaint was Starbucks' high coffee prices compared to regional drinks. These cultural and economic divides had to be addressed for corporate success. Starbucks worked with local firms to understand the Chinese market and customer patterns. This partnership helped them comprehend tea's cultural significance and alter their offerings.

After discovering that Chinese customers liked tea, Starbucks introduced many tea-based drinks to its coffee lineup. They adjusted their drink sweetness and incorporated regional favourites to suit Chinese tastes. Starbucks' designs reflected Chinese culture and aesthetics to provide welcoming gathering areas. Their stores were in crowded places to maximize exposure and accessibility. Starbucks respected Chinese culture by participating in community activities and supporting area organizations. They also trained store personnel to connect with culturally intelligent customers from diverse backgrounds.

The company invested heavily in in-store events and marketing initiatives to educate Chinese consumers about coffee culture, building a clientele that valued coffee as much as tea. Starbucks' culturally aware and adaptable strategy worked well. It overcame early criticism and established a strong brand in China. Chinese consumers welcomed the company since it blended in with local culture while maintaining its brand identity. By 2022, Starbucks' second largest market outside the US was China, with thousands of shops. Starbucks' success in China shows how cultural intelligence can help international companies succeed. Starbucks' success in China shows how cultural understanding and adaptability are crucial to global corporate success. Customizing products, recognizing regional customs, interacting with the community and educating clients about coffee culture helped the business grow in a foreign market. This case study shows how local customization and cultural knowledge may help multinationals succeed in foreign cultures.

Better Cultural Intelligence and Decision-Making

People with cultural intelligence are better able to comprehend and assess circumstances involving various points of view and to arrive at wise decisions in cross-cultural settings. People and groups can work together to find practical, mutually agreeable ideas that take into account various goals and viewpoints with the aid of cultural intelligence.

Increased Efficiency in Cross-cultural Agreements

To come to a contract, people and groups involved in global bargaining (such as those involving contracts) frequently have to work through intricate and drawn-out debates. Those groups with high CQ demonstrate more tolerance and a stronger capacity to persevere and work together across cultural and national boundaries to bargain and create advantageous, win-win contracts, regardless of whether these conversations include varied coworkers, customers or vendors. These fruitful outcomes stem from their capacity to comprehend and apply various points of view to the bargaining procedure.

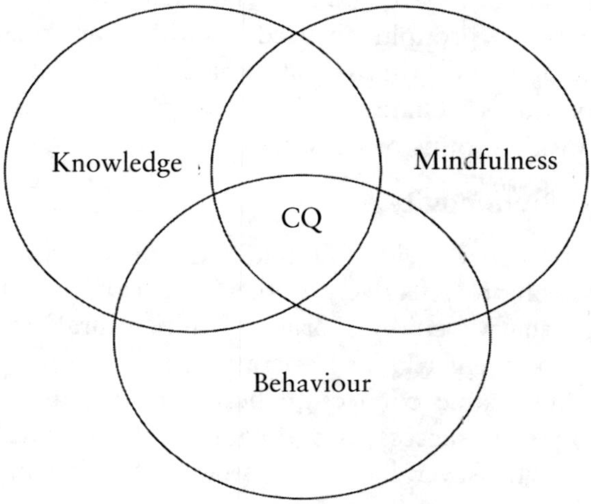

Figure 4.1: Elements of CQ

Source: https://www.researchgate.net/figure/Components-of-CQ-NOTE-CQ-cultural-intelligence_fig1_247738392

Increased Degrees of Data Sharing, Innovative Co-operation, Concept Sharing and Confidence

Research indicates that diverse multicultural groups prefer to function worse than homogeneous ones, even though diversity has an enormous opportunity to boost creativity and invention for people and businesses. This is especially true unless teammates have a high-level of intercultural proficiency. Increased levels of CQ among individuals and teams lead to a higher degree of knowledge and concept sharing, facilitated by the enhanced trust established among them. As a result, people and groups with cultural intelligence collaborate more creatively and generate more original ideas. Notably, among culturally varied groups of coworkers and/or partners, CQ tends to lower the perceived interpersonal dangers associated with speaking up. Because, CQ is positively correlated with confidence, culturally intelligent people and groups are more inclined to feel psychologically secure (strong CQ groups additionally embrace and integrate new members more quickly and have a higher degree of cohesiveness). The correlation between cultural intelligence and confidence is noteworthy, and it can be attributed to CQ's ability to reduce social grouping procedures that hurt relationships between people and groups from varied cultural backgrounds. These procedures include people classifying others as members of either inside groups or outsiders.

Enhanced Productivity

Contrary to people with minimal CQ, those with excessive CQ execute more effectively if their superior or subordinate has an alternative cultural origin. Multicultural groups that possess an excellent CQ also operate better than those that do not. The favourable connection between cultural intelligence and employment success in a range of cross-cultural settings is supported by several research studies. Significant CQ, for instance, has a positive impact on a variety of job performance outcomes, including job performance in culturally varied environments, adaptable achievement (such as the ability to modify actions to suit the needs of the circumstance or the surroundings), global management efficiency, revenue growth in cross-cultural or international environments and export achievement. Research published in the *Journal of World Business* found a positive relationship between an individual's CQ and their job performance, especially for those interacting with culturally diverse groups.

In summary, CQ denotes an individual's ability to navigate diverse cultural environments, encompassing dimensions like motivation, awareness and cognitive strategy. This adaptable skill can be enhanced through training and self-assessment, enabling individuals to excel in various capacities, from collaborating in multicultural teams to engaging in global negotiations. The origin of CQ lies in recognizing the imperative need for adapting to diverse cultures. CQ comprises three pivotal elements: meta-cognition/cognition, drive and action, emphasizing critical thinking, self-awareness and the effective application of cultural knowledge. Research shows that individuals with elevated CQ exhibit superior intercultural adaptation, decision-making and productivity, establishing it as a valuable asset in diverse professional landscapes.

Activity

1. Provide a definition of Cultural Intelligence (CQ) and expand on its interconnected characteristics.
2. Examine the importance of grasping the concept of culture in the context of improving intercultural competence.
3. Analyse the role of cultural knowledge within the CQ framework.
4. Investigate the three dimensions of CQ. Provide examples that demonstrate the fundamental role each dimension plays in developing an individual's proficiency in diverse cultural environments.
5. Examine how individuals exhibiting high CQ showcase the capacity to comprehend and evaluate situations that involve diverse perspectives in cross-cultural settings.
6. Explore the impact of Cultural Intelligence (CQ) on cross-cultural agreements.
7. Evaluate the contribution of CQ in cultivating a work environment that is more creative and unified.
8. Provide a concise summary of the primary benefits of Cultural Intelligence (CQ) for individuals, groups and companies.

5

Developing Cultural Intelligence: Cultural Dimension Models and Theories

Developing Cultural Intelligence and Theories

According to Thomas' interpretation of the cultural intelligence model, an individual can attain CQ by combining expertise, awareness and skills (as abilities). Individuals who possess cultural intelligence can apply their knowledge to comprehend various facets of cultural events that they encounter; they employ mindful cognitive methods that allow them to see and comprehend any given circumstance; and they build an ability repertoire that allows them to adjust and then exhibit suitable actions in a variety of contexts. These are the competencies most in demand in modern global business.

Knowledge is the ability to identify basic behavioural norms (rituals, customs, language, and so on) and to comprehend basic facts about the politics, economics, history and social environment of a particular culture. It is possible to comprehend the way one culture differs from another, the way that culture influences conduct, what a few of the core values of that culture are, or even a few of the basic rules for interacting with members of that culture. This is undoubtedly better than not knowing anything about a specific culture; that being said, it is insufficient to merely understand the customs of individuals, groups or the state. The complexity of human communication and the multitude of cultural nuances and reactions mean that mere possession of cultural knowledge—however noteworthy—does not guarantee competency. Even though it's a positive step, speaking another language well, for instance, cannot take the place of empathy for the opinions and actions of others. Everyone has encountered someone proficient in language but lacking in cultural awareness. One cannot automatically communicate politely and intelligently with individuals from different cultures just because they are proficient in one or more languages.

Nor does it follow that someone will automatically become culturally proficient just because they have had any amount of cultural interaction. Neither the length of time invested locally nor the experience of being overseas alone was found to be predictive of shift, according to the latest research examining the educational results of learners on educational missions overseas. Instead, what changed was the students' deliberate and active attempt to reflect on what was occurring—in real time—and then they modify their actions in accordance. Through the action of teachers, who challenged them to consider what was taking place and why it occurred, learners had the chance to acquire this ability set. This stands as the fundamental purpose of being mindful in learning about cultural differences, as depending solely on our devices might prevent us from prompting each other to understand the *why* behind the *what*.

Cultural Dimension Models

It is obvious that a business's culture has an impact on it and that the cultural disparities between the workforce and the clients/consumers it serves have a bigger effect on a business's accomplishment or failure.

Numerous sociologists, anthropologists and managerial specialists have presented their perspectives on culture through models that are outlined as follows:

- Florence Kluckhohn and Fred Strodtbeck
- GLOBE (Global Leader and Organisational Behaviour Effectiveness)
- Edward Hall and Mildred Hall
- Fons Trompenaars
- Geert Hofstede

Edward Hall and Mildred Hall Model

The six dimensions of culture that anthropologist Edward Hall and his spouse Mildred Hall have identified depend on their business expertise as well as numerous qualitative investigations.

- *Language of Time*: The two categories are further divided into Monochronic culture (also known as M-time) and Polychronic culture (also known as P-time). As time is as valuable as money, according to M-time culture, it shouldn't be abused in any way. Time thus receives greater importance than individuals. Whether it's a societal gathering, conference or schedule, individuals from M-time cultures are always on time. On the contrary, Polychronic cultures place a higher value on individuals or human connections than on periods.
- *Language of Space*: The term 'proxemics' is another name for it. The largest office usually belongs to the most significant individual. However, there are cultural differences in how people use their area as well.
- *Language of Things*: This aspect of culture highlights how members of a culture own material possessions.
- *Language of Friendship*: This dimension explains how individuals go about becoming friends. That is if members of a culture find friends readily, maintain those friendships for a long time, or break them readily and often. Generally speaking, not every culture values connection and relationship with an identical level of passionate fervour. A person's privacy and self-interest can take precedence over other considerations at times.
- *Language of Contracts*: Individuals from certain nations or cultures like things to be in black and white, particularly when it comes to contracts. Conversely, certain cultures adopt an entirely different strategy.
- *Two Types of Cultures, High and Low Settings*: High-context cultures emphasise implicit interaction, so understanding the setting is given more weight than understanding the words. The majority of information is left unspoken so that the recipient can deduce the

meaning for themselves by analyzing the setting and the words used. On the other hand, in low-context cultures, communication is explicit, meaning that phrases are given their primary significance, and the recipient is expected to comprehend the message solely from the words employed, disregarding the setting.

It was not stated that the dimensions mentioned earlier, which were acquired inclusively, were all-inclusive.

Florence Kluckhohn and Fred Strodtbeck Model

Six dimensions of culture were proposed by Kluckhohn and Strodbeck depending on issues that are common to all societies.

(*i*) What is someone's fundamental perception of and faith in another person?

(*ii*) How does an individual perceive their rights and obligations about the natural world?

(*iii*) What obligation does an individual have to other people?

(*iv*) What constitutes a society's primary mode of operation?

(*v*) How does a business company evaluate space?

(*vi*) What do individuals value more—the past, the present or the future?

Geert Hofstede Model

In the area of cross-cultural comparable studies, it was the initial significant investigation. The six widely recognised dimensions that Hofstede looked at are:

(*i*) *Power Distance Index (PDI)*: This dimension gauges how much the business's weaker employment acknowledges that authority is not distributed equally. The way society handles individual differences is the main issue with this.

(*ii*) *Collectivism versus Individualism* (*IDV*): Individualism denotes a lightly connected social system where individuals prioritise themselves and their close relatives. Conversely, collectivism suggests a close-knit societal structure where members genuinely believe that they owe it to one another to be loyal to one another.

(*iii*) *Masculinity versus Femininity* (*MAS*): The characteristics taken into account when determining masculinity are accomplishment, bravery, assertiveness and monetary rewards for accomplishment. On the other hand, the feminine component of this dimension encompasses values like humility, collaboration and concern for the fragile.

(*iv*) *Uncertainty Avoidance Index* (*UAI*): A low rating or value on the index indicates that executives and staff members of the business are more relaxed and risk-takers, feeling less reliant on formal regulations when faced with unpredictable circumstances. Conversely, an elevated rating on the index indicates the exact opposite.

(*v*) *Long-term normative orientation* (*LTO*) *as opposed to short-term LTO*: Individuals with a short-term perspective appreciate conventional ideals greatly and are norm thinkers. They think that rapid outcomes are important. Long-term thinkers, on the other hand, think that circumstances, settings and temporal factors all play a significant role in determining what is true. They have a strong desire to get outcomes.

(*vi*) *Restraint versus Indulgence* (*IND*): Indulgence is defined as a society that allows for the comparatively unrestricted satisfaction of fundamental human needs associated with having fun and enjoying existence. Contrarily, the Restraint constraint is a symbol of a society that imposes rigid societal norms and standards to suppress and regulate the satisfaction of requirements.

Fons Trompenaars Model

Throughout the 1980s and continuing for multiple decades, Trompenaars and Hampden-Turner conducted surveys with workers at different degrees of the hierarchy. They used seven criteria to categorise cultures:

(*i*) *Particularity versus universalism*: This refers to the criteria used to evaluate connections.

(*ii*) *Individualism versus Collectivism*: This assesses how much workers believe they work better as a group or as people.

(*iii*) *Emotional versus Neutral*: Is it appropriate to express feelings?

(*iv*) *Particular versus Diffused*: This describes how much accountability is given to a particular task or accepted.

(*v*) *Ascription versus Achievement*: This contrasts the degree to which a position is bestowed upon individuals and the amount to which they must demonstrate their worth to obtain it.

(*vi*) *Sequential versus Synchronous*: If individuals think that tasks should be completed one at a moment or in groups.

(*vii*) *Inner-directed versus Outer-directed*: This refers to how individuals approach, if they have managed over or are forced to co-operate with their surroundings.

GLOBE

In 1991, R.J. House led a multinational project involving 170 investigators from sixty-two different nations. It calculated the following nine cultural dimensions:

(*i*) *Performance Direction*: This refers to how much the community supports and honours individuals, when their performance improves.

(*ii*) *Ambiguity Avoidance*: This refers to how much a society, organisation or business relies on laws and societal standards, to reduce uncertainty about what will happen in the future.

(*iii*) *Humane Direction*: This index gauges how much society rewards people for being kind, unselfish, fair, giving and caring toward others.

(*iv*) *Institutional Collectivism*: This tells us how much the businesses value and promote group resource sharing and group efforts.

(*v*) *In-group Collectivism*: This refers to how much an individual expresses loyalty and pride in their households or businesses.

(*vi*) *Gender Egalitarianism*: This refers to how much society minimises sex disparities.

(*vii*) *Future Orientation*: This refers to how much the business's staff members embrace future-focussed behaviours like putting off indulgence, making plans and making investments in the years to come.

(*viii*) *Power distance*: This measures how much society's people anticipate an equivalent dispersion of authority.

(*ix*) *Assertiveness*: This refers to how much a worker displays aggression and self-assurance in interpersonal interactions.

Therefore, it can be said that while distinct anthropologists have developed different models about distinct aspects of culture, all of them emphasise the importance of understanding culture for a business to function successfully and efficiently.

In conclusion, the cultivation of CQ involves amalgamating expertise, awareness and skills to empower individuals in comprehending, utilizing mindful cognitive methods and adapting within diverse cultural contexts. The essential competencies of knowledge, awareness and skills play a pivotal role in navigating the complexities of the global business landscape. While possessing cultural knowledge is advantageous, it remains incomplete without a genuine empathy for and nuanced understanding of cultural intricacies. The significance of intentional reflection and active learning is underscored in the development of cultural proficiency. Diverse cultural dimension models, such as those proposed by Edward Hall, Florence Kluckhohn, Fred Strodtbeck, Geert Hofstede, Fons Trompenaars and GLOBE, provide valuable insights into the profound impact of culture on business success. Recognizing and integrating cultural understanding is foundational for fostering effective cross-cultural communication and collaboration in the dynamic global business environment.

Activity

1. Discuss the importance of intentional reflection and active learning in developing cultural proficiency.
2. Describe how individuals can achieve Cultural Intelligence as per Thomas' interpretation of the cultural intelligence model.
3. Examine the six universally acknowledged dimensions within Geert Hofstede's model. Explore their impact in cross-cultural business scenarios.
4. Investigate the cultural dimension models outlined in the text, including those by Edward Hall, Florence Kluckhohn, Fred Strodtbeck, Geert Hofstede, Fons Trompenaars and GLOBE. How do these models provide valuable insights into the influence of culture on achieving business success?
5. Summarise the fundamental lessons about fostering CQ and the crucial role of comprehending diverse cultural models in achieving success in global business communication.

Part III

Communication Styles Across Cultures

6

High-context versus Low-context Cultures

Introduction

A fundamental understanding of the social conventions and cultural standards that guide actions and choices is crucial for transnational businesses to compete more successfully. It could be the deciding factor between achievement and failure. A deeper comprehension of the communication preferences of Westerners and Easterners under stress is imperative, as evidenced by the March 2011 radioactive catastrophe in Fukushima, Japan, which was triggered by a tsunami. The administrations of Japan and other countries, as well as TEPCO (Tokyo Electric Power business), which is in charge of running the Dai-ichi Fukushima nuclear-powered plant, had a lot of misconceptions in the weeks and months that followed the accident. Nevertheless, the majority of cross-cultural misinterpretations are less obvious, often unnoticed and low-level. To understand how these types of cross-cultural disagreements develop and to draw attention to the fundamental standards that are present as cultural foundations or schema, intercultural communication concepts are a useful place to begin.

High and Low-context Communication

Participants from collective and distinctive cultures tend to favour certain fundamental forms of communication, which are explained by Hall's (1976) concept of low and high-setting culture. In line with this concept, non-verbal communication and included definitions discussed by speaker and spectator that heavily rely on setting are characteristics of high context (HC) cultures like

Japan. A high-context culture direction occurs, when every person of an identical category shares data in an identical way. This inclination for communication makes it possible for data to evolve and be updated, preserving a high degree of context and obviating the requirement for literal statements. Since the utterance possesses inherent significance connected to the context in which it is stated, the focus of the speech is on the *way* and *by whom*. On the other hand, low-context (LC) directed cultures (such as the US) are stated to admire literal, explicit communication between the participant and the spectator; in the Western culture, the significance of articulating one's views to avoid missing opportunities is encapsulated by the phrase, the squeaky wheel often gets the oil. In low-context cultures, the communication's particular topic is valued more and the setting is less important to more accurately anticipate the audience's actions during direct communication. Positive connections with people in the in-group setting are generally valued more in high-context cultures compared to low-context cultures.

Criticisms

From an educational perspective that only takes into account human comprehension and conduct, the HC-LC concept is indeed constrained and has come under heavy fire lately for doing exactly the reverse of what it is supposed to do—that is, creating harmful assumptions that lead to an increase in mistakes in communication and misconceptions. In that they seek to characterise a collection of traits that individuals within groups typically adhere to find definitions in particular circumstances, IC concepts are fundamentalist concepts. Conversely, from a non-essentialist standpoint, individuals extract from culture what they need to support their lives in diverse situations, recognizing the dynamic nature of culture. Moreover, a fundamentalist perspective seeks to describe the individual before comprehending the individual by using predetermined data (high/low setting). Though admirable, this way of thinking obfuscates IC in two ways as well. First of all, implying that 'we must consider each assertion of what they perform and state meticulously' when interacting with a person from a distinct experience is both literally not feasible and possibly naively distinctive. The vast majority of our communication is restricted by the deeply ingrained culture of unacknowledged prior expertise. Therefore, if we are unaware of Big C cultural standards and the way they are impacting our communication, it will be very hard, if not feasible, to change them. When faced with uncertainty, we use this presumptive knowledge—also known as cultural plan—to cover in the blanks. For instance, the Japanese speaker would use a highly context-focussed cultural plan to try to think through the effects a decision might have an impact on other members and connections within the collective before providing an assertive or direct response in a contentious face-losing situation. Equivocating statements like 'We are required to look into the matter more carefully' or 'I'm intrigued by what other people think' is HC for 'we are required to develop an agreement before establishing a decision'. It is one thing to say that all people ought to be comprehended on a one-to-one foundation. Putting this into practice becomes notably challenging in situations where crucial decisions must be promptly made, there is a lot at risk necessitating swift cross-cultural communication, or extensive public and private agreements worth billions of dollars are in jeopardy. The Western business traveller is distinguished by a firm adherence to a low-context (LC) cultural standard, a desire to achieve maximum efficiency in the shortest timeframe, and a clear preference for prompt and practical outcomes over prolonged, consensus-building, and face-saving discussions often associated with high-context (HC) standards that consider the needs of every individual within specific categories. Second, group norms and values—as well as the way they are embraced and regarded to various extents within a given community—are included in a description of culture. Ultimately, there's a reason why IC concepts have persisted for this long. They serve as helpful jumping-off indicates and heuristic tools to facilitate easier and more comprehensible cross-cultural communication. Perhaps the most effective way to conceptualise intercultural concepts like the high-low setting is as a range that people fall into at various stages in their lives, with certain people displaying more or less significant cultural traits than others based on the way specified in the setting. When the other speaker deviates from the embraced group standards of communication, this is known as distinct conduct. Furthermore, a lot of communication may be context-dependent, particularly if it's thought that broader cultural standards have been observed or satisfied.

English as an International Business Communication Instrument for LC

Thousands of people across the globe can now communicate in a language other than their native tongue and country of origin—thanks to the medium of English. It is acknowledged that using the English language for global business communication is essential. Japanese businesses that rely on conducting business abroad are hiring more people, who speak English fluently and mandating that this language be employed in conferences. Numerous sizeable multinational Japanese corporations, including Nissan, Uniqlo, Softbank and Rakuten, now require excellent command of English from both prospective and present staff members and keep conferences in that language. It seems that people are gradually realizing how important international ties are to Japan. English has become the preferred language for international communication not only due to the financial power of English-speaking nations but also due to the language's underlying cultural principles, which are especially supportive of clear and successful communication in international environments with an elevated level of confusion among speakers. Because it is an LC language, it fits perfectly to play this part. In the business world, interactions are often effective when there is clarity and limited opportunity to establish an environment.

As a result, using clarity and specificity to demonstrate one's honesty and reliability through communication, a low-context communication style requires being explicit and direct. Since their culture is primarily low-context, Americans, in instance, require and prosper on particularity. By using the LC cultural system, having items explained or expressed implies that we may prevent misunderstandings with individuals from different origins. High-context cultures—like those in China, Korea and Japan—place a high importance on social hierarchy, agreement decision-making and interpersonal balance. This encourages a more tactful, roundabout method of communication. High-context cultures are more tolerant of linguistic uncertainty than low-context cultures since language isn't anticipated to be complete in empty spaces; rather, the setting is anticipated to do so through the HC cultural structure. In this instance of business interaction between a native Japanese participant and an English participant, we observe how both low and high setting cultural standards may impact comprehension.

For example, in a particular business conference, both speakers interact (in English) according to their respective cultural standards. Mr. Otomo takes a high-context, consensus-building method, whereas Mr. Browning takes a feasible, direct method for LC. They are confused because neither party appears to understand the other or their communication preferences. Cultural position and layout dictate how language is employed and understood and are essential to understanding how a community constructs significance. When you are frequently needed by your language to provide specific kinds of data, it makes you pay attention to specific data in the external environment and to specific facets of expertise that participants of other languages might not always be expected to consider. Furthermore, since these speech patterns are developed from an early age, it makes sense that they could develop into mental patterns that extend outside language and have an impact on your observations, views, connections, emotions, recollections and sense of direction in the globe.

Case Study: English in Low-context Cultures

Japanese e-commerce and online retailing company Rakuten Inc. is a case study using English as an international commercial communication tool in low-context cultures. When it made English its official language in 2010, the startup Rakuten took a gamble known as 'Englishnization'. This choice was notable given Japan's high-context culture, where communication is often indirect and relies on shared understanding and non-verbal indicators.

Context

Rakuten chose English as its official language to be globally recognized. The firm sought worldwide e-commerce dominance to rival Amazon and Alibaba. Hiroshi Mikitani, the CEO, believed that adopting English as the company language was essential for innovation, international communication and talent acquisition.

All Rakuten employees, regardless of rank or location, had to meet a certain English proficiency level. The company set a deadline for staff English competence, funded language lessons, and rewarded individuals who met or exceeded expectations. The English language changeover changed the company's culture. Rakuten tried to alter its company culture from Japanese to global. This involves open communication and providing guidance to help reduce fear of making mistakes in English. By using English, Rakuten was able to hire specialists from around the world with diverse perspectives and skills, which is vital for innovation and worldwide expansion. English helped Rakuten's European, American and Asian operations. This was necessary for international collaboration, knowledge sharing and business planning. The Rakuten Englishnization effort yielded several notable results: English helped Rakuten enter new markets, work better with foreign partners and customers and operate more worldwide. The policy created a more inclusive and diverse corporate culture by making employees from different cultures feel more integrated. After executing its Englishnization policy, Rakuten partnered with and acquired firms worldwide, consolidating its position as the global e-commerce leader.

Rakuten's shift to English as its corporate language highlights its recognition of English's effectiveness in cross-border communication, especially in low-context cultures. This case study explains how a non-native English-speaking corporation can promote a more unified, imaginative and competitive global enterprise by overcoming international business communication challenges. Rakuten's success shows how important English literacy is in the global economy, especially for high-context cultural firms going global.

The Pros and Cons of HC-LC in International Business Environments

A high-context method is challenging in the international business environment where English is a form of communication until both high and low-context-directed individuals are cognizant of their own sub-consciously influencing communication standards that influence their responses and communication. When interacting with HC-oriented participants, LC might sense unreliable and insincere orientation, even though HC-oriented communication cultures frequently view LC participants as immature, anxious or rude to others. Japanese businesses operating abroad frequently lament that they don't receive sufficient data from Japan to a degree where they start to question whether data is being withheld from them on purpose.

These misconceptions, which also fully materialised in the wake of the Fukushima nuclear accident, are founded in the unconscious cultural schema. Furthermore, Western LC businessmen have a generally an adverse opinion or consensus, even though it is an extremely desired practice in HC cultures like Japan. It is helpful to take into account the presumptions and shortcomings that both the HC and LC cultures render to combat these kinds of unfavourable conclusions.

In summary, a profound comprehension of cultural norms is essential for global business competitiveness. Understanding communication nuances in high and low-context cultures is crucial for effective information exchange. Despite criticism, the high and low-context model remains a valuable tool for navigating cross-cultural interactions. While English serves as a universal business language, the contrast between high and low-context styles presents challenges. Successfully, recognizing and navigating these cultural dimensions are crucial for global communication and success in international business endeavours.

Activity

1. Define and expound on Hall's concept of high-context (HC) and low-context (LC) communication cultures. Explore the influence of these cultural orientations on non-verbal communication, information sharing, and the importance of explicit statements in various societies.

2. Explore the influence of cultural norms on communication. Offer examples illustrating how cultural norms are utilised in decision-making and responses within distinct cultural contexts.
3. Investigate the influence of cultural context on communication in the realm of international business. Compare how a communication style with low-context differs from high-context communication.
4. Analyse the advantages and disadvantages of high-context and low-context communication in the context of international business environments.
5. Provide a concise overview of the essential observations concerning the significance of cultural norms in global business competitiveness, the complexities of high and low-context cultures, and the advantages and challenges associated with international business communication.

7
Direct and Indirect Communication

Introduction

The modern globe has shrunk to the size of a worldwide village, with data moving at the rate of light and little separation between places. We appear to be a part of this worldwide village every time, we read a magazine, watch television or make a grocery purchase. Because of this, even though we may not travel the globe, it occurs to us, because we engage in international interactions and trade through various communication modes.

To meet the demands of modern society, communication has evolved and/or revised, but it has also grown more complex. Known as 'the essential foundation of societal encounter', it is utilised in all facets of our lives, including work, play and personal relationships. Even if the procedure of sending and obtaining data is straightforward, misinterpretations or breakdowns in communication may result from the significance that it conveys and how it is interpreted. As previously mentioned, 'when it involves finding out what goes wrong in life, communication breakdown is by far the most prevalent clarification'. For instance, identical investigators contend that insufficient human interaction, as evidenced by sub-par co-operation, sub-par management or interpersonal conflicts, is more often the cause of challenges in businesses than scientific or managerial difficulties.

Intercultural communication presents a greater challenge than intercultural communication within one's own culture, because mutual codes and conventions are either obsolete or incomplete. Culture affects communication and inversely, so cultural disparities between the interlocutors endanger communication through lowering the accessible standards and practices shared. These distinctions are significant and impact individual capacities for communication, because they function at every stage of behaviour, verbal and non-verbal.

According to one of the multiple meanings of culture that have been proposed—and the one that is based on Hofstede's theories-–culture is a collection of shared mental initiatives that direct and affect people's behaviour. It appears that though deeply ingrained mental initiatives regulate such behaviour, culture is related to daily conduct. Stated differently, culture directs people's lives. Individuals make their own decisions as people, but they do so within the constraints imposed by the cultures in which they live.

One culture seems to be taking centerstage and influencing every other one on the global scene of today. The English language has emerged as the *lingua franca* of international education and business and American culture has spread to nearly every country in the globe through mass media, McDonaldization and usage. Numerous individuals envision a merging of cultures around the globe.

On the other hand, the slow rate of change is a major obstacle to internationalisation and convergence. Culture is prone to evolve and convergence likely takes effect only in superficial issues like business practices and certain customer tastes despite the globe's swift modernization and transformation. Furthermore, modifications can be frequently reframed to align with prevailing cultural norms.

As previously stated, culture affects how people communicate both inside and outside of our community. One widely recognised and extensively researched contrast in communication styles is that between direct and indirect.

Indirect and Direct Communication

Some cultures communicate more indirectly than others, especially those of the Middle East and Asia. Individuals are more concerned with preserving face and preventing humiliation in these situations, so the environment is of greater significance—for instance, the physical environment, the previous connections among individuals and non-verbal behaviour than the subject matter. The degree of inherent and mainly sub-conscious awareness an individual may be anticipated to bring to a specific communication environment is the subject of situation theory. Due to their familiarity with one another and their understanding of how communication works, interlocutors therefore infer significance to avoid upsetting anyone and preserve equilibrium.

Conversely, cultures that emphasise the core of the communication—the words—rather than the environment, choosing to speak the truth and employ explicit, direct, obvious verbal statements, are found at the other extreme of the spectrum. These cultures are typically Western ones. Since the emphasis is on honesty, truthfulness and the sharing of literal data, interlocutors do not need to look between the sentences or search for implicit significance, because they express what they intend precisely and *vice versa*.

A common connection between the communication environment and the dichotomy in communication styles is the significance of maintaining one's face. The correlations are stronger still: direct communication is common in low-context, heterogeneous, individualised and low-power-distance cultures, while indirect communication is typically seen in high-context, uniform, collective and high-power-distance cultures.

While this categorization is straightforward, real-world circumstances and cultural norms are more difficult to categorise. There is communication between the two severe ends of the continuum. Based on the circumstances, individuals from their own cultures employ both forms of communication. However, as the studies checked in the intercultural area indicate, the propensity to favour one style of behaviour over another is extensively stated to differ across cultures.

This implies that when individuals with distinct communication styles interact, miscommunications and misinterpretations could occur, because established norms and codes can shift, become unforeseeable or become perplexing.

Furthermore, comprehension in face-to-face communication can be aided by actions and explained by inquiries or recurrence; however, writing presents more challenges. E-mails are one such instance, which relies heavily on taking turns and hardly ever allows for implicit significance.

Being capable of communicating in a distinct style from the one that is familiar may occasionally require learning another code to comprehend the various communication styles. This suggests that on-the-job training is required. One can learn a new code on their own, through studying and expertise, or from instructors in official environments.

Case Study: Nuances of Direct and Indirect Communication

The global leader in assurance, tax, transaction and advisory services, Ernst & Young (EY), is the subject of a case study on communication issues and both direct and indirect communication. One excellent example of navigating cultural communication barriers is EY's efforts to enhance internal communication and collaboration among its ethnically diverse workforce.

Context

People of many cultural backgrounds work at EY in more than 150 countries. Its workforce's diversity presents advantages and difficulties, particularly in communication. Because of their global reach, EY teams typically comprise professionals from direct and indirect communication cultures, such as the US, Germany, Japan and India.

Ensuring effective and efficient communication among team members with varying communication preferences was EY's largest challenge. While indirect communicators favour harmony and may employ more intricacy, direct communicators place more importance on simplicity and clarity. These differences led to conflict, inefficiencies and miscommunication within the team. EY provided cultural competency training, with a focus on comprehending and adapting to a range of communication styles, to all employees. Included were useful exercises on reading non-verbal cues and interacting well in multicultural environments. EY intentionally assembled teams of individuals from a variety of ethnic backgrounds to introduce staff members to a range of communication styles. Team members were able to modify their communication style based on this experience. To communicate across time zones, EY made use of technology. Apps for instant messaging and project management were utilized to lessen misunderstandings brought on by different communication styles. Team members were able to constructively resolve conflicts and misunderstandings with the aid of well-defined and organized feedback systems. This tactic encouraged open discussion on communication difficulties and preferences, which led to continuous development. Effective direct and indirect communication was a consistent trait of EY executives. Leaders, who communicate with empathy and agility motivate their staff.

Results

EY's comprehension of communication styles and bridge initiatives produced many outcomes. As teams grew more cohesive and effective, misunderstandings declined and output rose. When workers felt appreciated and understood, their level of engagement and satisfaction rose. Improved team dynamics fostered innovative concepts and solutions. By managing communication issues and providing top-notch services across cultural and market boundaries, EY strengthened its position as a worldwide leader.

Difference Between Direct and Indirect Communication

Those who communicate directly often express their opinions. Their phrases are the main means of communicating their message and they rely on the true significance of these phrases. Obtaining or providing data is the main objective of communication. Low-context cultures, which are typically more culturally diverse and prioritise individuality, autonomy and self-reliance, frequently communicate directly. There are no extensively held beliefs regarding the setting in which communication occurs as a result of this diversity. It is the speaker's responsibility to communicate clearly in direct communication.

In indirect communication, which is prevalent in high-context cultures, significance is expressed not only through words but also through non-verbal cues like stops, silences and tone of speaking, subtlety, consequence and general comprehension of the communication's setting.

Upholding equilibrium and preserving face is the central objective of the communication transaction. Conflict, strain and awkward circumstances are things that indirect communicators try to stay away from. Deep and frequently sub-conscious comprehensions of societal norms are developed by individuals living in high-context cultures, which can be rather homogeneous and stress independence and societal connections. Since there are common standards regarding conduct, the speaker can change the setting to communicate a message.

Things that communicate data include the speaker's personality, communicational components omitted and non-normative actions. To comprehend the significance of indirect communication, the recipient must be culturally aware. Understanding the content is the audience's responsibility; thus, the awareness and the capacity to grasp the under-the-surface significance and to detect the implicit significance becomes essential. Stereotypes concerning the two communication styles may be clarified by using proverbs and other expressions taken from the resources listed below.

Critique of indirect communication is widespread, particularly in the US. According to Tannen, "several Americans consider it obvious that openness is rational and linked with authority while indirectness corresponds to lying and displays subservience", highlighting a widespread "mistrust of indirectness". Indirect communicators can be perceived by direct communicators as fraudulent, passive-aggressive, fragile, deceitful and unclear, false and unreliable, and they anticipate and appreciate truth and directness.

Furthermore, the task of successful communication appears to fall on those who are indirect in the United States; data is perceived as being communicated by the indirect communicator instead of being understood by the listener.

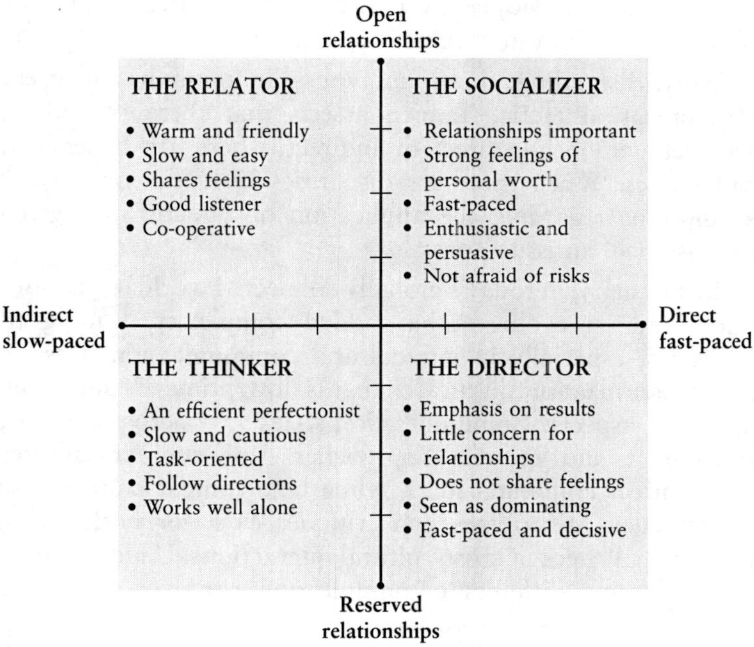

Figure 7.1: Direct versus Indirect

Source: https://foxhugh.com/multicultural/direct-versus-indirect-communication-style

'Those who anticipate indirection will be annoyed by talking in a different method', as stated by direct communicators, also have problems with indirect communicators. People may view direct communicators as impolite and unsuitable, which can cause stress in relationships, harm to one's image, the impression that one is performing poorly and other issues. In essence, direct communicators are unaware of what they're lacking and how indirectness functions. 'Until we are completely submerged in indirectness, it is very difficult for a direct individual to completely comprehend its difficulty' (Ananaria). Direct communicators frequently overlook nuances and subtleties like the expression of critiques. Due to this, direct communicators may experience frustration and confusion while operating in indirect surroundings. They may be aware that something failed, but they are unsure of what they could be doing incorrectly, and since they are enveloped by indirect communicators, nobody will directly point out their mistakes to them.

Notwithstanding these unfavourable opinions of every communication tactic, Tannen asserts that there is nothing incorrect with being direct or indirect. There are benefits to both tactics. When there are disparities in tactics or varying assumptions regarding the application of a tactic in a given circumstance, an issue arises.

In summary, in today's globally connected world, communication and its evolution has added complexity, leading to challenges, especially in intercultural communication. Despite rapid modernization, cultural change is slow, primarily impacting superficial aspects. Communication styles vary across cultures, with direct and indirect approaches. Low-context cultures favour direct communication, while high-context cultures use indirect cues. Stereotypes and critiques exist for both styles, creating challenges in cross-cultural interactions. Understanding and navigating different communication contexts and styles require cultural awareness.

Activity

1. Examine direct and indirect communication approaches. How do these approaches differ among various cultures? Offer examples of cultures that tend to favour more indirect communication and those that emphasise direct communication.
2. Examine the statement that 'communication breakdown is by far the most prevalent clarification' for challenges in businesses. Illustrate instances where misunderstandings or failures in communication can lead to issues in organizational settings.
3. *Consider the statement*: Culture directs people's lives. Investigate how culture impacts decision-making and behaviour, and emphasise the significance of acknowledging cultural factors in global business interactions.
4. Explore the difficulties and advantages of adopting English as the primary language for international business communication. Evaluate how proficiency in the English language impacts business interactions within a global context.

5. Reflect on the obstacles associated with e-mails and written communication, when bridging the gap between direct and indirect communication styles. How can individuals modify their written communication to convey messages effectively in diverse cultural contexts?

8

Non-verbal Communication in Different Cultures

Non-verbal Communication

The term verbal communication describes communication that takes place via the use of phrases. Thus, verbal connection implies oral contact and verbal proof implies oral proof. Language-free communication is referred to as non-verbal communication. The standards for non-verbal communication differ from nation-to-nation and even within a single culture, just like they do for other facets of communication.

The ability to observe is directly related to non-verbal communication. The speaker must be seen to, audible to, and perhaps felt by the recipient of the communication. The person receiving the communication ought to be able to properly view the speaker's facial expressions, posture, voice, clothes and look, as well as hear their accent. Non-verbal communication can be both intentional and accidental, because it is observed. It is intentional, when the speaker makes an effort to communicate with the target audience by using deliberate gestures, stances and various non-verbal cues. Whenever the recipient interprets the speaker's body language, stance or look particularly whenever it is not conducted deliberately, this is considered unintentional non-verbal communication. Despite the presenter's sincere intentions, a casual stance or outfit might well be mistaken for a lack of concern. Another universal non-verbal behaviour is smiling, though different cultures have different reasons for smiling. Although there are increasing non-verbal resemblances between cultures due to the spread of Western media, especially in the US and other Western nations, the most significant cultural variations in non-verbal communication relate to touch, eye contact and private space. According to a study by UCLA (it is a public land-grant research university in Los Angeles, California), a staggering 97% of workplace communication is non-verbal.

Benefits

1. To transmit information relating to charts, maps, infographics, and so on. Due to non-verbal techniques' ability to condense a lot of information into a little package, the recipient can comprehend the situation at a look.
2. Since drivers and pedestrians should react immediately to road indicators and signs, non-verbal communication seems crucial.
3. Generally speaking, people react to noises, colours and visuals more rapidly than they do to any speech.
4. The only way to communicate with those who cannot read or write is by using non-verbal signals.

Body language

Body language refers to shifts in posture and motion that reflect a person's emotional state. Most people are not mindful of their body language, thus a large portion of it is mindless and involuntary. However, it has a significant influence on others.

There are two types of body language: Unconscious and conscious

1. Unconscious motions have a biological basis and are influenced by cultural traditions and developed habits.

Biological

People have particular movements, attitudes, and postures due to their body types, skin tones and facial features. Additionally, we continually work to conform our bodies to the surroundings, which might or might not be pleasant.

Habitual

In the course of adjusting oneself to the surroundings, certain gestures become learned as habits. They can also result from a job that needs continual motion or particular postures. It's also a professional tendency to use particular verb tenses and expressions.

Culture-specific practices include not crouching down in front of seniors and not staring them directly in the eyes. A few actions are also part of societal behaviour, greeting practices and introductory practices.

2. Intentional motions, stances and speech modulations are made. The utilization of body language is something that performers are specifically educated in, as well as strong speakers and particularly effective speakers.

Although no one can fully regulate their body language, it is essential to increase body consciousness and have a fair degree of control over their stance, motions and voice tone. We can better comprehend the body language of others if we become more aware of our body language.

Looks

Various factors affect a person's overall looks. Hygiene and personal grooming are two of the key elements that affect attractiveness. The quality of care for the face, fingernails, toes and hair is required. A person, who ignores these facets comes across negatively. First impressions are formed by looks; unkempt look, negligence in grooming and awkward clothing leaves a bad one. An unkempt look readily reflects a poor condition.

Facial Gestures

Body language is a highly expressive and complex tool used by some cultures more than by others. Generally speaking, the north Europeans and Asians are viewed as having more reserved gestural communication styles, whereas Italians and other Mediterranean people fall into the former group. It is commonly stated that the expressions displayed through body language or facial gestures are generally considered universal, with the underlying premise being that conveying fundamental feelings is an essential, natural trait shared by all people.

The indicator of the mind, so the saying goes, is the face. The face frequently displays the emotions of the heart and the ideas of the intellect. The mind-set, emotions and response of the speakers can be expressed by the use of words or non-verbal facial gestures, such as a happy or appreciating smile, an angry frown, a surprised glance and many other facial gestures. Some individuals have a talent for interpreting facial emotions. Effective communicators acquire to read and understand facial expressions, whether they are the presenter or the audience.

Eye Contact

A crucial component of facial conduct is eye motion, which is used to attract focus and express astonishment or enjoyment, among other emotional expressions. To show that both parties are involved in the conversation, the presenter and audience must make eye contact. When giving an oral speech, it's crucial to make eye contact with the listener to establish a connection.

Speakers consider it a goal to scan the entire group using one glance, creating fleeting eye contact with as numerous people as they can. Eye contact should only be maintained for three to five seconds at most, as maintaining it longer than that can be uncomfortable for the other individual. Although it's generally accepted that minimizing eye contact shows that a presenter is dishonest, certain liars may maintain unwavering eye contact while waiting for your reaction. People, who lack assurance frequently avoid making eye contact. Nevertheless, cultural norms and practices have an impact on the ways individuals utilise their eyes and faces.

Refusing to make eye contact is regarded as a respectful gesture in certain cultures. Nevertheless, this avoidance of eye contact might be interpreted as an indication that the other individual is being unkind, deceitful or bored. Certain Native American tribes advocate for avoiding eye contact with instructors, elders and other individuals in positions of authority. Unaware of this custom, educators may interpret a Native American learner's failure to make eye contact as an indication of insubordination or disengagement, which can cause problems in the educational setting by giving the wrong impression that the learner is a troublemaker or not very smart.

Smile

One of the most effective facial expressions is a smile. It makes communication possible. A genuine, nice grin plays a significant role in forging and maintaining human connections. *The proverb*: 'You are not completely clothed until you carry a smile' beautifully highlights the importance of smiling.

Body Postures

In terms of stance, we mean how someone stands, sits and moves. The posture of the feet, hand, and various bodily features exposes not just a person's mental condition, such as if she or he is lively, active and energetic, tense and jittery, strong and self-confident, and so on, but additionally her or his command of the communication's topic. An effective presenter maintains a straight back, her or his feet close, her or his balance precisely over the instep and her or his chin parallel to the ground or at a perfect angle to the spine. Speaking in front of an audience successfully requires that you stay in this position. A presenter, who has a postural tummy and sagging shoulders appears to be exhausted.

Your character is also displayed by the way you sit. A group discussion member will adjust her or his stance, when it is her or his turn to talk. Nevertheless, various circumstances call for various stances. Both feet can be on the ground, one just in ahead of the other, and the back can remain straight from the hip up.

The way someone walks might reveal their level of assurance or reticence, vigour or withdrawal.

A presenter must keep in mind that to step elegantly, they must keep their legs free at the hips, lift their feet off the ground when walking, keep their gait straight, and avoid strides or little movements.

It goes without saying that to communicate effectively, a person must learn where to put their hands while communicating, how to change their stance and transfer their body mass from the back to the legs.

Gestures

When communicating effectively and producing useful material, gestures, are crucial. The presenter's mental condition might well be revealed by gestures like fidgeting with jewellery, tightening a key chain or firmly clasping one's hands, which can alter both the decoding and encoding of her or his content during the conversation.

A person is most likely holding up their middle and index fingers, if they are from the USA or Great Britain. You are most likely holding up your index and thumb, if you are not from a different European nation. Some Europeans begin calculating on their thumb and finish with five on their pinky finger, whereas Americans and British begin calculating on their index finger and finish with five on their thumb.

A skilled communicator develops suitable gestures by practicing them in front of a mirror. Additionally, he or she asks his or her friends and coworkers for advice in this area. But when employing gestures, one must always be self-assessing, examining and applying the proper gesture for the appropriate influence. It is likewise essential that one must exercise caution and attention, when making gestures, because of cultural restraints, sexual connotations and ethical obligations. While gestures certainly add significance to communication, if they are not utilised with consideration for the period, location and person involved, they might become uncomfortable. Some examples of gestures: a greeting, a sitting posture, a thumbs-up, a hand-to-face gesture, a collar draw, thumbs and finger rubbing, eye indicators, an eye blink, and so on.

When employing gestures, we should exercise caution even when they are common in culture and might be interpreted as universal. Several European cultures consider the OK sign, which consists of a circled thumb and index finger with the remaining fingers spread, to be offensive. It originated in North America. Similar to this, in Australia and England, making the peace sign with two fingers pointing inward is considered offensive. In North America, the thumbs-up gesture denotes a job effectively accomplished; in Greece and other places, it is akin to the derogatory "Up yours!" President Bush of the United States is well-known for using the Texas Longhorn soccer group's "hook 'em horns" signal to express his support for the College of Texas marching troupe. That gesture is widely recognised in Italy, yet it fails to convey let's rock or fan enthusiasm. Il cornuto means that the other individual is a cuckold, meaning that his spouse is having an extramarital affair.

Accessories

Body language is heavily influenced by apparel. Achieving a subtle influence through your attire requires a sense of discretion. The dress is comprised of colour, style, cut and fit. It is appropriate to dress in either national or modern fashion in India, giving us a variety of options. It's important to dress appropriately for the event. The formal gathering, the time of day, the seasons, the individuals, who would be in attendance, their cultural backgrounds, and your own firm's traditions must all be taken into consideration. The choice of clothing accents like ties, shoes and jewellery, ought to be precise and they must be at ease. Accessories consist of a purse or briefcase.

Capacity

Although it can be difficult to express enthusiasm and power as a part of body language, many individuals have felt the influence of someone, who exudes a lot of power. Body language is greatly influenced by one's bodily and psychological wellness; a healthy individual is active and retains a particular degree of enthusiasm at employment. The manner of a person reflects their passion, which is frequently contagious and causes audiences to get enthused as well.

Chronemics

The monochronic direction of the US and of numerous north and Western European nations is to view moments as a resource that may be planned, preserved, utilised and discarded. Events must have a defined start and finish time and be planned. Mexico and Spain are two examples of nations with a polychronic direction to duration. It may be unattainable to arrange an appointment timetable in an orderly manner due to scheduling conflicts. Additionally, people might forget time constraints or global meetings without saying sorry, which would be viewed as extremely impolite by someone with a monochronic direction to duration. When individuals from polychromic cultures reject global meetings or shut down businesses due to family-related reasons, individuals from monochronic cultures get irritated. On the other hand, individuals from polychromic cultures believe that US Americans, for instance, prioritise their timetables over their interpersonal connections.

Proxemics

Each speaker has created or developed a particular area and territory around themselves, which they do not let others enter during communication until the presenter and recipient have a close connection. According to Edward T. Hall, there are four different types of range in human relationships:

1. Up to 18 inches of close physical interaction
2. *Individuals*: 18 inches to four feet.
3. *Societal*: Four to 12 feet.
4. *Audience*: 12 feet for hearing and visual range

Without a doubt, each of these four categories has a different kind and level of communication activity. Yet keep in mind that we each choose these places for ourselves and that we could alter them by moving. They are therefore unique to us as individuals. Space separation varies from culture-to-culture. The communication process and the contents of the signal can occasionally be harmed by space distance. The usual distance, meanwhile, can be disregarded in a psychological state that is emotionally intense.

To summarise, effective communication involves both verbal and non-verbal dimensions, with non-verbal cues, such as body language, facial expressions, eye contact and gestures playing a pivotal role. Understanding the cultural nuances that influence non-verbal communication is crucial for accurate interpretation. The skill of observation is directly linked to the ability to grasp and respond to non-verbal signals. In professional contexts,

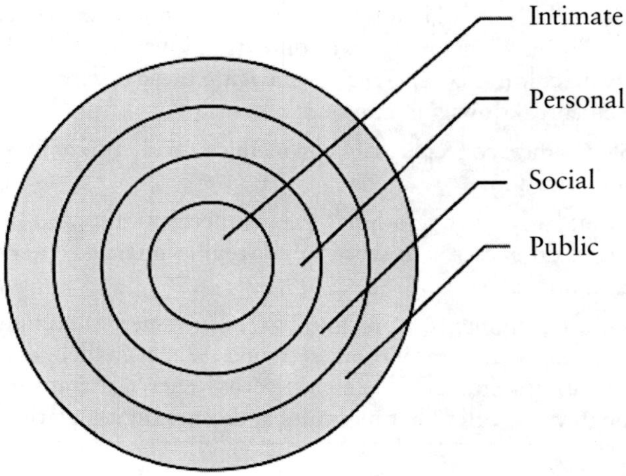

Figure 8.1: Hall's Proxemics Zone

Source: https://www.Researchgate.Net/Publication/348554450_Digital_Proxemics_Approach_In_Cyberspace_Analysis_-_A_Systematic_Literature_Review#Pf2

where non-verbal communication holds substantial weight, being attentive to both intentional and unintentional cues is paramount. Furthermore, elements like body posture, facial gestures and overall appearance significantly contribute to forming initial impressions, highlighting the necessity of mastering these non-verbal aspects for successful communication.

Activity

1. In what ways do non-verbal techniques, including gestures and facial expressions, contribute to a more effective understanding of the message?
2. How expressions such as smiles, frowns and raised eyebrows are interpreted in various cultures, and how can understanding these interpretations improve cross-cultural interactions?
3. Explore Edward T. Hall's classification of spatial relationships in human interactions. Investigate how spatial separation influences communication dynamics and how individuals can adjust their utilization of personal space in varying situations.

4. Explore the potential misinterpretations of non-verbal cues, especially in diverse cultural contexts. How can individuals cultivate cultural competence to navigate these differences and prevent breakdowns in communication?
5. Explore the concepts of chronemics and proxemics in communication.
6. In what ways can clothing impact perceptions, and what function do accessories serve in conveying nuanced messages in communication?
7. Discuss the influence of technology on non-verbal communication, especially in virtual settings. What challenges and opportunities emerge, when non-verbal cues are transmitted through video calls, chat messages and other digital platforms?

Part IV

Language Barriers and Solutions in International Business

9

Impact of Language Differences on International Business

Introduction

The functioning of Multi-national Enterprises (MNEs) and foreign subsidiaries has long been the subject of study in international advertisement, as has the function of language in customer study, advertisements, buying goods and services, marketing and global market possibilities and selection evaluation. Not only does language serve a crucial function in oral and written communication as well as data supply, but it also has an effect on human capital, which makes it indispensable to international business.

Unified expertise and data lead to mutual comprehension through the procedure of communication. We begin by taking into account language as an independent idea and then following recent advances. Even though language plays an important role in international business and advertising, it has been neglected and relegated to the status of the overlooked variable in multinational administration, because it is seen as part of the culture. But with three distinct perspectives on language, the latest profusion of studies has taken language outside the culture set.

We view language as a means of co-ordination and communication between agents. Gaining proficiency in a single shared framework for interaction, comprehension, co-operation and communication is the foundation of pertinent language expertise. Businesses that operate abroad frequently interact with linguistically diverse settings. Assessing and calculating the degree to which the language setting in the nation of origin differs from that in the nation of origin has been used in efforts to measure language differences (LD).

We operationalise LD by looking at the language(s) that MNEs communicate in both their residence and host countries, as well as language connect (the percentage of the host populace that can communicate the substantial languages of the MNEs' home nation), language disparity (the degree to which the MNEs' primary languages vary from one another), and English application in the host nation. We will determine the pathways via which LD affects affiliated efficiency, drawing on research on language in MNEs.

Impact of Language Differences on International Business and Marketing

Information can be expensive in an international environment, and LD exacerbates information imbalance even more. Thus, proficiency in a language is necessary for efficient information sharing and communication both within an international business and with its business partners.

Communication and data movement are hampered by language barriers, which can cause opposition, dissatisfaction, disputes and distrust. Language may serve as an instrument of identity, authority and exclusion, which can lead to these problems. Speaking a language other than their mother tongue makes them less confident and easier to understand, when communicating in that language. This can make it harder for them to participate in business operations and increase the likelihood that they will be unintentionally or purposely left out of the decision-making procedure. If there is LD, this would affect the exchange of data and communication between an affiliate and other parts of the MNE, when it comes to the business degree. In a similar vein, language proficiency can put users in an area of authority, enabling them to access additional assets or take on the role of data barriers by purposefully obstructing, slowing down or altering the transmission of vital data. To distinguish insiders from visitors, societal limits as well as mental and operational obstacles may be established along linguistic lines. Therefore, communication and data movement would be more difficult for branches, whose native language differs from that of MNEs.

The ability to successfully handle and operate a business depends on its human capital, which can be undermined by language barriers. International groups are unable to completely comprehend their tasks due to confusion stemming from language barriers. This leads to unresolved needs, causing team members to appear unpredictable and compromising the group's overall effectiveness. In addition to potentially hindering an employee's performance, language barriers can lower the significance of a professional's ability in the eyes of their peers. The lack of language competence of the HQ managers/expats in their home nation can be interpreted by subsidiary employees as a sign of an absence of charm, trust and leadership abilities, undermining their power and guidance.

An interpreter with a high degree of expertise in the specialised field may be required as a quick fix to fully utilise the human capital of an individual with constrained language competence for communication. This could result in significant additional expenses.

It's interesting to note that although language is a fundamental aspect of the scientific setting in international business, administration, and advertising, the idea of language has only recently come to play a major role in scholarly study. The impact of language has been emphasised in a lot of studies in the areas of international customer behaviour, business marketing and buying, branding and advertising, service advertising and international advertisement communication. It has also been discussed which language must be employed, by whom, and under what circumstances. Studies of international market prospects or selection evaluation have underscored the significance of linguistic factors in determining the allure and reach of overseas markets. The marketing field has also noted that foreign language proficiency is just as crucial as sales aptitude when hiring salespeople.

More specifically, LD can have an extensive variety of business effects on foreign affiliates of MNEs. Previous research has determined the detrimental effects of LD, such as impeding the exchange of data, knowledge movement and communication, generating disputes in the connections between headquarters and subsidiaries, and affecting foreign direct investment and international mergers and purchases. Furthermore, LD adds to the liability of foreignness (LOF). These language impacts may eventually have an important influence on business performance.

Case Study: Impact of Language Differences on International Business

South America, Asia and Europe have been seeing a rapid increase in the services offered by GlobalTech Solutions. The business takes great satisfaction in its creative solutions and customer-focused methodology. But as it expanded into other markets, the linguistic barriers started to present serious difficulties, impacting every facet of its business operations, from customer service to product localisation. Their major issues were:

- *Communication with Clients*: In non-English speaking nations, many clients prefer doing business in their tongue. Client discontent stemming from inadequate understanding or meeting of their needs led to misunderstandings and delays in project timeframes.
- *Internal Communication*: Workers from various linguistic backgrounds made up GlobalTech's diversified workforce. The absence of a common language occasionally led to misunderstandings and ineffective teamwork in its international operations.
- *Product Localisation*: Originally, the company's marketing materials and software were solely offered in English. As a result, user experience and adoption were hampered in markets where English was not the primary language.
- *Legal and Compliance Issues*: Language difficulties made it difficult to comprehend and abide by the legal requirements of many nations, which raised the possibility of noncompliance and possible legal issues.

To address these issues, the company started offering its staff language training, with an emphasis on the languages of its main markets. Furthermore, cultural sensitivity training assisted staff members in appreciating and comprehending the subtleties of the cultures in which they worked. The business employed native speakers of the pertinent languages who understood the customs and regulations governing doing business in the area. This enhanced both client communication and adherence to local laws. GlobalTech invested in tools and software for language translation to improve communication among its international teams and to improve product localisation by translating its marketing materials and software into many languages. The company also set up multilingual customer care centres so that customers could get help in their native tongues and increase customer satisfaction. Results: Higher customer satisfaction and retention rates resulted from improved communication and the opportunity to serve customers in their preferred language. By enhancing internal cooperation and addressing language hurdles, effective worldwide operations and project delivery were achieved. The company was able to establish itself more successfully in new areas, all thanks to its products that were tailored for various markets and its increased proficiency in navigating legal and cultural intricacies. GlobalTech's all-encompassing strategy for handling linguistic variations turned into a differentiator that set it apart from its rivals who had not sufficiently addressed these issues.

International Subsidiary Performance and Language Differences

In this part, we will integrate the growing body of study on language in MNEs with the in-depth analysis of affiliate performance to discover the pathways through which LD impacts performance. Initially, LD has an impact on performance because of how it functions in the flow of data and communication.

Horizontal, vertical and diagonal communication both within and between businesses is essential to the achievement of a contemporary MNE.

Successful interaction helps an affiliate perform well by lowering transaction expenses, improving functioning efficacy and effectiveness and obtaining promptly useful market data. LD makes the flow of data and communication more difficult and expensive. Language barriers can be reduced by using translators, contemporary communication techniques, language instruction and bilingual staff who serve as language intermediaries between speakers of various languages. Large proof, however, indicates that LD still causes total loss, deformation (which means directed significance is changed during transfer) and data filtering (information is just partly passed). Staff dissatisfaction, disputes and opposition in an affiliate are further consequences of miscommunication. Staff performance, which is based on their ability to engage in significant and suitable communication in their professional interactions in both intra- and inter-organisational contexts, effectively defines the performance of the business.

Additionally, LD can distance the connection between an affiliate and its HQ, thereby reducing communication and interactions within the MNE. This isolates the affiliate and lessens the advantages it receives from the HQ. Language ability has an impact on MNE internal communication. When there is linguistic diversity, there are fewer visits from top administration to affiliates. When language is used as an origin of authority, affiliates in a host nation where the legal business language or the language of the MNE's nation of origin may hold a place of authority within the MNE system because they have accessibility to more assets and authority than they would have otherwise.

Multinational enterprises encounter external obstacles linked to language barriers when engaging with regional vendors, clients and numerous other outside parties, including local authorities, oversight organisations and associations for advocacy. MNE affiliates are more likely to have participants from diverse backgrounds because of their international nature, which makes them vulnerable to international disputes. When the parties present are unable to interact efficiently, these disputes can escalate and have a detrimental impact on performance. For instance, when communicating in a language other than their native tongue, buyers seem less assured and courageous and are less inclined to conclude profitable agreements, while salespeople seem less competent, trustworthy, likable, and eventually less convincing.

LD affects how decisions are made. Executives communicate and carry out plans through language. When there are several languages spoken, information needs to be interpreted. Hiring qualified interpreters and translators increases the expenses of the project because they need to put in extra work and be paid. As a result, decisions are made more slowly and inefficiently, and tasks and processes take longer, incurring additional expenses. Senior administration is aware of the negative effects language-related communication and decision-making issues can have on the work output. In a 2011 investigation by Forbes Research, 106 top managers at big US companies were asked about miscommunication. The results showed that 67% of respondents thought this caused ineffectiveness, 46% thought it complicated cooperation, and 42% said that language barriers prevented them from being as productive as they could be. Lastly, more than 80% of respondents said that when supervisors spoke to their staff members in their mother tongue, the response rate and productivity increased.

Secondly, because of its effects on information dissemination and transmission, LD may harm affiliate performance. Affiliations frequently benefit from the transfer of assets from MNEs, which are typically of an intangible and tacit natural world. Since knowledge is not a neutral, freely flowing resource, transferring information is an exhausting procedure that involves several factors, including the recipient's ability for absorption and learning goals, the integrity of the connection, causal confusion and the source's appearance. Even in situations where communication is adequate, LD may prevent subsidiaries from understanding and assimilating implicit knowledge. It would be even more difficult for affiliates to gain from the information that is accessible to them in the event of inadequate communication. Evidence currently in existence has demonstrated LD's detrimental effects on international comprehension dispersion and transmission. Better performance results from sharing information, but language barriers make it difficult to transmit expertise, which lowers affiliate performance.

Finally, learning non-native languages raises LOF. Investigations have demonstrated that LOF lowers performance. The drawbacks of an MNE affiliate's experience in a host nation are known as local onshore finance LOF. It results from a prejudice risk or a lack of acquaintance with the surroundings of the country of origin. MNEs look for credibility when investing in a host nation because it gives them the ability to conquer LOF and aids in realizing value gain in business operations.

But LD puts MNEs up against obstacles like the ones mentioned previously. Consequently, it has a detrimental effect on the performance of its subsidiaries. It is customary to employ a prevalent language fake, which focuses on the MNE's native nation and the host nation where both communicate the identical language. But merely considering if the residence and host countries speak the same language would fall short of fully capturing LD. It ignores the fact that a multilingual nation has speakers of multiple languages, albeit in varying percentages.

As a result, there are variations in the degree of language overlap between nations that share a prevalent language; Canada and Switzerland, for instance, share English. Nonetheless, compared to Switzerland, a larger proportion of people live in Canada and communicate in English. Because there is a greater possibility of direct communication with English speakers in Canada compared to Switzerland, UK MNEs are prone to have a greater level of language simplicity there compared to Switzerland. Additionally, a portion of the populace in the nation of origin might communicate languages from their country of origin even if there isn't an important language spoken by both.

The language barrier that MNE activities must overcome will be lessened if a sizable section of the populace in the host nation communicates the languages of their nation of origin. We restate our main theory with reference to linguistic overlap.

Language learning may be used to get over language barriers in situations where nations do not speak the same language or languages. What matters is how simple or complex learning a second language is. The structural variations among languages that are largely culturally inert have been examined by linguists. In terms of language household connections, certain languages are more alike than others; that is, there are differences in the language distances between language groups.

Languages from the same family are typically closer, possess an identical syntax, and are less difficult to acquire and comprehend than languages from other households. Similar to this, languages from an identical subbranch of the same family can sometimes comprehend each other and are also simpler to learn. This claim has been supported by scientific research, which demonstrates that participant second language competency increases with decreasing linguistic distance from their native tongue. The difficulty of learning a foreign language increases with linguistic separation. Greater language barriers will therefore probably impact affiliate performance.

A lingua franca can serve as a bridge language between an MNE's residence and its host activities where there isn't a prevalent language. Presently, a lot of MNEs conduct business in English, and an increasing number of MNEs from non-English speaking nations choose to employ English as their business language. This is related to English's widespread usage as the language of choice. Due to internationalisation and the diversity of cultures that use English, the language has become much more widely used globally, which has resulted in a laissez-faire attitude toward English transactions.

Most of the human understanding is preserved in English documents, making English the most extensively discovered second language (L2). Additionally, individuals can now transition from speaking their native tongue to English in numerous different nations. The intra-language impact of English makes international interactions easier between nations with various languages as well as between English-speaking nations. The majority of human understanding is preserved in English papers, making English the most extensively learned L2. Additionally, individuals can now transition from speaking their native tongue to English in numerous different nations. The common adoption of English in a host country can improve affiliate performance because English promotes international trade not just between English-speaking nations (the intra-language impact of English) but also between nations that communicate various languages (the inter-language impact or lingua franca impact). There are 2 methods in which this may be expressed from the standpoint of LD between the language of the nation of origin and English. The initial concern is if the nation being hosted speaks English. The subsequent approach is to use the language separation model and consider the gap between English and the primary language of the host nation.

To sum up, language plays a crucial role in shaping the intricate dynamics of international business and marketing. Its influence is widespread, moulding communication patterns, knowledge exchange and overall organisational effectiveness within the realm of MNEs. LD introduces varied challenges, impacting both internal and external communication and potentially resulting in misunderstandings, conflicts and reduced efficiency. The concept of LOF further highlights the obstacles MNEs encounter while manoeuvring through global markets due to linguistic differences. Strategic approaches, such as adopting a lingua franca or considering linguistic overlap, provide practical solutions to enhance the performance of international subsidiaries. A nuanced comprehension of the language's role is essential for MNEs, enabling them to adeptly navigate the intricacies of global communication and attain optimal results in diverse linguistic landscapes.

Activity

1. Explore how language variations affect external interactions with regional vendors, clients, and other stakeholders in the context of international business.
2. Define the concept of LOF and elucidate how language differences contribute to LOF in the context of international business.
3. Discuss the potential challenges and benefits associated with the common adoption of English in host countries.
4. Examine potential strategies to address language barriers, including the deployment of interpreters and bilingual staff. Evaluate the associated costs and benefits of these solutions and analyse their impact on the overall efficiency of international business operations.
5. Define the role of language in MNEs and foreign subsidiaries

6. Analyse how language barriers affect the transfer of information, the movement of knowledge, communication between central offices and branch locations, and the execution of international mergers and acquisitions.
7. Examine the concept of a lingua franca and its role in international business. How does the adoption of a lingua franca such as English impact communication and interactions within MNEs, especially when engaging in business activities in countries where English is not the primary language?

10
Strategies for Overcoming Language Barriers

The definition of language administration is "the degree to which the organisation can meet its language requirements by wisely implementing a range of language management instruments, such as language instruction and expatriation". Global businesses do not need to provide a single approach to achieve the most effective cooperation dynamics. Rather, they can use a variety of language management strategies inside the business's regulations to address communication issues. The key is to identify which current approaches work most effectively in the setting of the business or to combine a couple of them to find novel possibilities.

The following pointers is a collection of the most widely utilised language management strategies in businesses:

- Employing regional agents to address linguistic issues
- Building web pages that are language and/or culturally appropriate
- Employing language inspections
- Employing qualified interpreters and translators
- Translating sales, marketing and/or technical content
- Providing cultural presentation programs and language instruction such as online language studying
- Putting in place 'polyglot' regulations for hiring and staff choice
- Promoting cross-border employee movement
- Implementing 'buddying' and 'secondment' programs

- Establishing connections with nearby colleges that accept international position learners
- Promoting the hiring of native speakers and organising multilingual e-commerce (for instance, using regional currencies and languages)
- The interpretation by machine
- Language Nodes
- Inpatriation
- Expatriation
- Selected Employment

Strategies for Overcoming Language Barriers

Language Training

The first place that businesses look to when they notice an expertise gap among their staff members is personnel development. Since language training is frequently employed as a managerial strategy in the corporate world, the training sector is highly established and provides a broad variety of language classes at distinct proficiency degrees. Nevertheless, since it is impacted by the business's financial status, language training programs are difficult for businesses to sustain over the long term. When a business is doing well, funds are allocated to training; however, when budgets are rigid, training is viewed as an initial privilege that must be forgone.

Many programs are offered in businesses to help employees become more proficient in languages. Businesses often implement extremely broad classes, sometimes referred to as quick fixes. Oftentimes, the outcomes are disappointing. It has to do with the fact that momentum and self-commitment are necessary for successful language acquisition programs. Since they understand that they need to acquire the language in its entirety before they can see any enhancement, students in broad classes lack the drive. The probability of not finishing these classes seems substantial, and they are discouraging and extremely difficult. Introducing the business to specialised learning, which focuses on appropriately recognised language requirements, is the solution to this issue. Customised programs are created especially to meet the business's set standards for communication. These classes seem to be highly advantageous. First off, workers benefit from their devoted work because they can put their newly gained information to quick usage. Consequently, the desire to learn is impacted and it continues to be strong. The program's ability to assist learners in making incremental improvements is another benefit. This is made feasible by the smaller number of realistically difficult yet difficult goals that have been set.

It is well known that the Volkswagen Corporation is at the forefront of language instruction. By using the six phases of the program, it handles language professionally and gets the worker ready to reach a respectable level of communication competence. The program has extremely rigid demands for fulfillment; every phase requires ninety hours of in-class research time in addition to more hours of independent study spread over six to nine months. Each participant must pass an accomplishment evaluation after every phase. To proceed with the training in subsequent phases, this stage must be finished.

Language Auditing

The procedure of determining the business's advantages and disadvantages when it comes to communicating in foreign languages is known as language auditing. It helps businesses to recognise the skills of their current workforce and their level of proficiency in particular areas. The goal of language auditing is to establish the requirement at a strategic threshold, but the procedure calls for financial assets, human resources, education and time commitment.

An Altered Form of Language Auditing Known as Language Check-up

There are a few disadvantages to language auditing, including the substantial costs and time commitment involved in the procedure. It also necessitates consulting outside language experts. For these causes, an alternative approach known as language check-up, which is a component of the linguistic audit, occasionally takes the set of the audit. The primary benefit of utilizing language check-up is its cost-effectiveness, as it can be self-administration without a requirement for outside language testers. The quicker production of outcomes compared to a typical language audit is another advantage. In addition, a language check-up addresses more language issues than an audit does. It specifically looks at the state of business language standardised procedures, computer structure reach, whether materials and web pages have various language interactions, and how often exterior language assets and translation instruments are used.

Language Barrier Aspects

The method for assessing the 3 aspects of language barriers in an organisation—language diversity, language entry and sophistication—is language auditing. Language Diversity is the total several of languages that an organisation speaks and understands to conduct business. Businesses that have partnerships, affiliates, vendors, consumers and other stakeholders spread throughout the globe must weigh the number of these to be conscious of the various languages that other businesses might speak. While Microsoft is a worldwide corporation that handles more than eighty languages, worldwide networks should be able to communicate in a multitude of languages, especially the languages of European nations and other languages like Chinese, Japanese, Arabic and some Asian languages.

Counting the operational domains within international businesses that function across language barriers is known as language penetration. Whereas the novel unified platforms touch almost every department in the organisation, cross-lingual communication used to be overseen by a small number of language experts. At this time, communication across language barriers is necessary for every degree and activity within each division of the business.

Analyzing language proficiency and needs based on an employee's division, status and role within the organisation is known as language sophistication. For example, secretaries must be able to handle conferences and comprehend fundamental messages. They are additionally required to be proficient in speaking and listening so they can respond appropriately to inquiries.

A stronger command of the language, proficiency in reading and writing, and the ability to work with a restricted vocabulary are all prerequisites for logistical accountants. To develop theories and solve written and verbal design challenges, international layout designers must be fluent in the language to the point where it is not a barrier to them. One of the most important skills for an international manager to have is outstanding language skills. Together with being adept at all the abilities necessary for communication—writing, speaking, reading and listening—they also need to possess the rhetorical abilities of humor, bargaining, persuasion and inspiration.

Lingua Franca

Since English is the standard language for business communication, businesses use it as a lingua franca as a part of their language administration strategies. Consequently, those who are not native people employ it. It is widely recognised that English serves as a *contact* language between delegates and staff from various cultural and linguistic backgrounds. The foreign language that has been selected to facilitate communication between businesses with disparate first languages is English. Dependency on a single language does have certain disadvantages though. For example, certain businesses claim the right to operate in the language of the client, which is why they ignore the growing pattern of utilizing multiple languages—languages that will eventually challenge English's hegemony.A further drawback of speaking only English during bargaining is that agreements and laws are almost constantly written in the regional tongue, which increases the likelihood of challenges for the speaker. When a business lacks proficiency in the regional languages, it becomes prone and powerless.

Operational Multilingualism

By employing actions, a blend of languages and various available means, the parties intend to convey their message. Nevertheless, depending solely on this trial-and-error approach might not be adequate and may not be the optimal choice in business discussions. Studies show that a cocktail of languages is used in 16% of international business transactions. Operational multilingualism has the drawback of potentially resulting in cognitive divergence amongst the participants in the discussion.

Exterior Language Resources

Businesses that expand their operations to foreign countries need people with the critical abilities of translation and interpretation. As a result, they turn to outside language resources, which can help them break down communication barriers. Whatever the scale of the business, building global relationships is essential for bolstering an entrepreneur's standing in the marketplace. The company faces a significant problem in providing translators with the setting of the subject matter, even though outsourced interpreters and translators aid in the coordination of international operations. The integrity of the business and customer connections may be hampered by the translator's ignorance of the good, the technology employed in manufacturing and internal business procedures. Their lack of business knowledge impacts the importance of third-party translators."Nothing functioned effectively and it was all expensive", as the Senior Planner employed to describe the business's utilization of translators, highlighting and revealing every fact about it. The assistance of translators cannot overcome or substitute the language barrier; therefore, their function must be employed with care. Using a translator limits the company's ability to operate to its maximum efficiency and efficacy and comes at a hefty expense.

Corporate Language

Another language management tactic employed by businesses is corporate language. Staff members are frequently required to undergo language training to ensure that their proficiency in the language is appropriate. The practice of designating one or more languages as the legal way of communication within an organisation is known as corporate language. Global corporations that offered numerous advantages, including Siemens, Daimler-Chrysler, Electrolux and Olivetti, implemented this approach into their policies. It standardises the official documentation and day-to-day correspondence with the business's affiliates and divisions. The ease of accessibility to data systems, policies, process papers and technical papers is another advantage. The second benefit is that it fosters a feeling of community and establishes a corporate language.

But there are a lot of disadvantages to this solution. The fact that it is a long-lasting strategy—meaning that the advantages won't become apparent until much later—is one of its main drawbacks. Implementing a single language may be challenging for a variety of justifications. For example, Nestle faced difficulties selecting the official language since its staff was undecided between English and French. The issue of staff members who are not proficient in the selected language is the final flaw in this approach. The number of employees with language abilities must be taken into account when choosing the primary language for the business, as inadequate understanding for the staff could result in opposition on their part.

Selective Recruitment

Hiring individuals who already have the necessary abilities is the most cost-effective way to address the language challenge. Put differently, the language barrier may be readily overcome by implementing Selective Recruiting. Nonetheless, the plan calls for the redistribution of employees and the potential for redundancy for those unable to handle their foreign language proficiency to the necessary degree. As a result, there are three distinct and varied scenarios in which the solution of employing selective recruitment ought to be used. First and foremost, it ought to be applied in contexts where language proficiency is seriously lacking. Secondly, when bringing in foreign supervisors. Thirdly, when establishing language nodes.

Expatriate

One quick fix for getting past language barriers is to employ this language technique. The language nodes created by these expatriate initiatives improve connections and communication between divisions and the corporate level. This solution's drawback is that it will cost more, which suggests that an international supervisor's pay will be more than that of a regional supervisor. Furthermore, because the expatriate supervisor must forge a novel identity in the new place, this approach fails to entirely address the issue of a language barrier.

Code Switching

Since it is nearly unattainable to learn a foreign language with native-like competence, people who speak it as a second language are conscious that their comprehension abilities could be deceiving. Since it is crucial to understand every aspect when conducting business, code-switching frequently occurs during meetings. Staff members desire to refer to their notes at crucial points to confirm that they comprehend the subject matter. For staff members who speak a second language, it may seem effortless and helpful, but for others who do not speak the language, it may be unsettling and give rise to suspicions of collusion or dishonesty.

In essence, language management in organisations includes strategies, such as training and expatriation. Various methods encompass employing local representatives, developing culturally suitable websites, language inspections, utilizing interpreters, translators and hiring multilingual staff. Personalised training proves more effective than generalised classes in overcoming language barriers. Language auditing identifies strengths and weaknesses, with a cost-effective alternative being language check-ups. Evaluating language barriers involves examining diversity, penetration and sophistication. While English as a lingua franca is widespread, operational multilingualism might lead to cognitive divergence. External language resources are crucial but may lack industry expertise. Corporate language designating specific languages for official communication has its downsides. Selective recruitment, where individuals with language skills are hired, offers a budget-friendly solution. Expatriation, involving international supervisors to create language nodes, incurs higher costs. Although code switching during meetings is common, it can elicit feelings of unease and raise suspicions.

Activity

1. What is the impact of English being used as a lingua franca in communication between individuals with varying linguistic and cultural backgrounds in the context of global business?
2. Discuss the importance of utilizing regional agents as a means to address linguistic challenges in multinational corporations.
3. What are the ways in which diverse language management strategies can be utilised to rectify communication challenges within an organization?
4. Explore how language auditing contributes to strategic decision-making in language management.
5. Investigate the utilization of code-switching as a coping strategy for language difficulties in international business meetings.
6. In what ways can tailor-made language training programs designed to address specific communication requirements contribute to the success of multinational enterprises?
7. Explore the difficulties and benefits of introducing 'buddying' and 'secondment' strategies as solutions to language-related challenges in international business contexts.

11
Role of Translation and Interpretation

Translation and Interpretation

A translator is someone who facilitates communication between speakers of various languages or who translates written material like a work of literature or speech into another language so that others can comprehend it.

A translator does more than just convert phrases between different languages. Acquiring proficiency in two or more languages is not a prerequisite for being a translator. This is due to individuals with diverse cultural origins requiring more than just language vocabulary and grammar knowledge to be effective translators. The subsequent attempts is to clarify the translation occupation from the viewpoints of various translators with varying language and cultural origins.

Translating entails breaking down language barriers and, to the greatest extent feasible, bridging cultural divides. It entails adopting a new perspective on the globe. I deal with individuals from all over the globe as a translator. Each of them views existence and other things differently. Therefore, when working as a translator, use more than one eye.

A powerful man or noblewoman who translates from sources to the intended language is called a translator. He or she works as political investigators as well. Presidents and sophisticated politicians use interpreters when speaking. Interpreting is a vital task, and your elegant translation might just save the day.

The aforementioned reasons make it clear that a translator acts as a liaison between two distinct languages and cultures. In addition to being a translator, an intercultural communicator is someone whose job is to build bridges and help people get over language and cultural barriers. For this reason, a translator needs to be an expert in a variety of areas, including translation, interpretation, task planning, service buying and managing international communication procedures. Indeed, translations serve as a bridge between previously disparate cultural groups to forge enduring relationships. It is therefore clear why translations are now so crucial, and a translator is someone who does more than just translate words; she or he are someone who can determine the best method to convey the primary concepts so that their target demographic understands them. It is also important for her or him to contemplate the political and societal context of the translation.

The goal of translation is to make something comprehensible for those who cannot comprehend the original language by acting as a stand-in for it. It is a strain on the translator to bear this great duty. A translator of employment from a various national culture must possess a fundamental understanding of history.Being merely proficient in the vocabulary and grammar of a foreign language is insufficient to qualify as a translator. Before making an effort to create a connection between them, one should have a deep understanding of both their own culture and language as well as the culture of the language they are speaking.

It is necessary to clarify the distinctions between a translator and an interpreter for people to comprehend their roles during the procedure of communication. Both have a lot in common and have a strong connection, but they also vary greatly from one another. They both translate from a single language into another, but they also vary in several ways.

The majority of individuals are aware that translation is not a literal translation but rather maintaining the initial significance of the source material. Even though the words are frequently distinct, they have identical significance. Unexpectedly, many mistakenly believe that interpretation is the same as word-for-word transcription. Frequently, an interpretation is a condensed form of the original text.

Examining the aforementioned points reveals that an interpreter and a translator share many characteristics. Still, there are distinctions between these two experts as well. The primary distinction between the two professions is that an interpreter works with spoken language, whereas a translator works with written materials, such as instructions, Internet pages, programs, legal, technical or medical papers, and so on.

Translation is the act of translating a factor that is composed, whereas interpretation is the process of translating something that is spoken. It is frequently necessary for an interpreter to translate back and forth, or from one language into another. Translators don't need to translate from one language again into a unique one; instead, they typically only translate into one language.

Interpreters must provide right away translations at seminars and conferences, broadcasting of signing for the hard of hearing, diplomatic negotiations between countries, calls via video or voice, and other events. They must pay close attention to what is being said, take notes and translate it into the intended language right away. Translations can be provided even after the original text was written. As a result, a translator has a lot more time to complete the translation, which allows them to be more exact and produce excellent results. Interpreters must thus depend on their education, encounters and understanding since they must translate right away. Translators have a greater opportunity to conduct online searches, use dictionaries, style instructions or even seek assistance from others to produce a precise translation than they do when they lack the ease of referencing resources. Once a translation is finished, for instance, it is usually sent to an editorial for accuracy checking; however, an interpretation process does not follow the same protocol.

Utilizing computer-assisted translation instruments, translators can produce their best work, thus innovation is often beneficial to them. Since they do not have the opportunity to access such resources, interpreters do not have such facilities. Regarding accuracy, there's another distinction between interpreters and translators.

While interpreters must preserve an extremely excellent standard of accuracy in their profession, it is permissible for them to have somewhat lower accuracy since the focus is on communicating the information without changing its significance. They are free to omit certain portions of the speech since it isn't always essential to translate every word. On the contrary, a translator is not free to select which parts of the source document to translate or leave untranslated. Instead, they must translate the whole file.

A specific writing style must be followed by translators; there are distinct forms of writing for technical records, legal, instructions for use, health reports, screenplays and other publications. The translator must also pay attention to punctuation. But, an interpreter doesn't have to be concerned about any of these things; instead, their main concern is matching the speaker's tone, modulation and inflections, which are essential in spoken communication. The listeners can learn a lot from these spoken hints.

Case Study: Role of Translation and Interpretation in International Business Communication

TechGlobal, a multinational technology company that expanded into Japan, illustrates how translation and interpretation improve cross-border business communication. This case study shows how effective translation and interpretation can overcome intercultural communication challenges and ensure company success.

Context

TechGlobal, a US software development company, markets extensively in Japan due to its strong economy and high demand for cutting-edge technology. However, linguistic and cultural differences hindered TechGlobal's agreements, cooperation and operations. The biggest challenge for the company's team was connecting with potential Japanese partners, clients and staff due to the language barrier between English and Japanese. The company initially lacked a deep understanding of Japanese culture, which was necessary to understand Japanese corporate structure, negotiation methods and business etiquette. Legal and regulatory compliance required precise technical language skills and legal experience to translate legal documents and ensure Japanese law compliance.

Resolutions

TechGlobal engaged experts to translate e-mails, contracts, proposals and promotional materials. This ensured that every document was translated appropriately, capturing Japanese business formality and product technicalities. They hired bilingual, tech-savvy interpreters for critical lectures and meetings. This enabled the company and its Japanese partners to communicate in real-time, fostering trust and understanding. TechGlobal taught its staff about Japanese corporate culture, emphasizing consensus-building, hierarchy and business card passing. This preparation established trust and a strong first impression. I worked with a local international business law firm to navigate the complex regulatory landscape and ensure that all contracts and business operations followed Japanese law.

Success

TechGlobal entered the Japanese market utilizing similar methods, creating connections with local enterprises and gaining a large clientele. Translation and interpretation services improved communication, avoided misunderstandings and strengthened relationships with clients and partners. The company earned its Japanese partners' confidence and respect by following Japanese business etiquette, which is highly valued in the Japanese corporate culture.

The methods of interpretation and translation are both delicate. As a result, it is critical to select the right phrases and communicate them in a suitable language to avoid any translation errors.

Role of Localization and Cultural Adaptation in Translation

In our interconnected global landscape, the ability to communicate seamlessly across diverse linguistic and cultural boundaries is not just advantageous but imperative. Translation stands at the forefront of this linguistic exchange, but its efficacy is deeply intertwined with the concepts of localization and cultural adaptation. Beyond the literal transference of words, successful translation hinges on the artful navigation of cultural nuances and the tailored adaptation of content. This introduction delves into the pivotal role played by localization and cultural adaptation in the realm of translation, exploring how these twin pillars amplify the impact of cross-cultural communication and bridge the gaps between languages and customs. Some important factors related to the localization and cultural adaptation are as follows:

- *Preserving Cultural Nuances*: Translation is an art that extends beyond linguistic conversion, encompassing the delicate task of preserving cultural nuances. Localization ensures that the translated content not only communicates accurately but also resonates with the cultural intricacies of the target audience.
- *Tailoring for Local Markets*: Adapting content for specific markets involves more than just language translation. Localization considers local preferences, societal norms and legal frameworks, ensuring that products or services seamlessly integrate into the cultural fabric of diverse communities.
- *Effective Communication*: Cultural adaptation enhances the effectiveness of communication by embracing the nuances of local cultures. This involves an in-depth understanding of cultural references, idioms and contextual subtleties, enabling the translated content to convey not only the words but also the cultural context.
- *Mitigating Misinterpretation*: Accurate translation is a safeguard against misunderstandings. Localization plays a vital role in mitigating the risk of misinterpretation by addressing cultural differences, thereby ensuring that the intended meaning is conveyed without distortion.

Ethical Considerations in Interpretation

Within the field of interpretation, ethics serve as crucial principles that assist professionals in navigating intricate scenarios where conflicting interests may emerge. Interpreters face challenges, including how to reconcile the imperative for precise communication with the protection of confidentiality, how to navigate cultural subtleties without displaying bias, and how to sustain impartiality while interpreting information that is sensitive or controversial. Some important factors related to the aspect of ethical considerations in interpretation are as follows:

- *Confidentiality and Privacy*: Interpreters are entrusted with sensitive information during their work. Upholding confidentiality and respecting privacy are paramount to maintaining trust, ensuring that any information shared during interpretation remains confidential.
- *Impartiality and Neutrality*: Maintaining objectivity is essential in interpretation. Interpreters must remain impartial, refraining from expressing personal opinions or biases, thereby ensuring that the interpretation remains neutral and unbiased.
- *Cultural Sensitivity*: Interpreters must navigate cultural differences with sensitivity. Understanding and respecting diverse cultural norms help interpreters foster empathy, contributing to smoother communication and mitigating the risk of cultural misunderstandings.
- *Professionalism and Competence*: Ethical interpretation demands a high standard of professionalism and competence. Interpreters must strive for accuracy, adhere to ethical standards, and continuously enhance their linguistic and cultural proficiency to meet the dynamic needs of diverse communication settings.

In essence, a translator facilitates communication between speakers of different languages and translates written material. Being a translator goes beyond language proficiency, requiring an understanding of cultural nuances. A translator works on written materials whereas an interpreter handles spoken language. Localization and cultural adaptation in translation is critical, emphasizing the need to preserve cultural nuances and tailor content for specific markets. Additionally, ethical considerations in interpretation, such as confidentiality, impartiality, cultural sensitivity, professionalism and competence, are crucial principles for interpreters to navigate complex scenarios.

Activity

1. Examine the role of a proficient translator, particularly in political environments. How does translation influence the outcomes of political investigations and diplomatic negotiations?
2. Why is it essential for translators to consider the political and societal context of their work?
3. In what ways have computer-assisted translation tools impacted the effectiveness and precision of translation tasks?
4. Why it is essential for interpreters to stay informed about language trends, cultural shifts and changing communication norms?
5. Explore the ethical considerations surrounding cultural biases in the interpretation process.
6. Compare the time-related challenges encountered by translators and interpreters in their respective fields.
7. Discuss the importance of maintaining neutrality and objectivity in interpretation.
8. Explore the role of localization in managing cultural distinctions and preserving the precision of intended meaning.

Part V

Effective Written Communication in International Business

12

Business Writing Styles Globally

To stay in touch with the outside environment, which includes other businesspeople, clients and governmental agencies, we are required to create business letters. Additionally, they can be used for corporate purposes, such as workplace instructions, circulars, memos, and so on. For a local firm, producing a letter might not be as crucial, yet it still has value.

There are other forms of communication as well, such as the telephone and telegraph, yet they could just leave a brief effect on the recipient. These media decrease the likelihood that the content will be retained in mind over a period.

The primary method of communication is through sending business letters. Business letters continue to be significant in corporate communication amid the widespread use of e-mail for internal and external communication. A business letter includes all of the benefits of written communication, such as that it may be preserved and referenced at any time and is a binding regulatory record.

The format of a business letter differs from that of a personal letter. This chapter suggests reviewing business letter composing fundamentals with learners because a business letter symbolises the company.

Business Letter Function

- The business letter is a document that can be referred to in the future. Back references are common in corporate communication. Just that whenever past activities, contracts, and so on involving users, providers and the kind are maintained in writing, they could be accessed conveniently, promptly and accurately.

- It is employed to broaden the region of activities because it may approach any place and makes a long-lasting imprint on the recipient's consciousness than oral communication.
- It functions as a regulatory record.
- It is employed to generate goodwill.

Different Letter Types

Personal writings are casual and are used to convey information or seek acceptance; writing to friends and family are examples of personal letters. Personal writings are composed in a pleasant, casual tone. When non-personal letters are employed for commercial purposes, they must be composed formally. The specific form is determined by the firm. There are several types of non-personal or business letters:

On a large scale, the accompanying is commonly utilised in organisations:

1. Official letters are typically sent to official or semi-government organisations.
2. Demi-official notes (D.O.) have an official function yet are issued to a specific individual by title. If a situation needs the addressees to personally handle it, if it is private, or if it is important and needs to be resolved right away, a D.O. letter might well be prepared.
3. Both administration and corporate organisations employ inner memos or letters for inner communication.
4. Form letters are employed for correspondence that is of frequent or repetitive character. They serve as a reference for the pertinent information included in this letter, such as acknowledgments, notifications, interviews, notices and appointments.

Elements of Business Letters

1. *Heading*: For communication with external parties, the majority of business firms employ their printable letters. The name, location, mobile number, and if applicable, the telegraph contact information are all listed on the letterhead.

The address and name are typically placed at the upper central core of the sheet with any other details being specified in the margins.

2. *Date*: Certain letterheads have a printed line that indicates where the date must be entered, while others allow the writer to decide where to put it. It needs to be entered 2 places after the letterhead's final line. On the top right side, the date, month and year ought to be written as

- 2nd August, 2001
- 2 August, 2001
- August 2, 2001
- (Of the 3, only the last two choices are accurate.)

3. *Reference*: 2 sentences are sometimes included on letterheads to list citations:

Offer the citation number over the 2nd sentence and the correspondent's citation number over the initial if you are responding.

Some businesses chose to include the correspondent's citation number in the letter's body.

4. *Internal address*: When there is no focus sequence or section above the greeting, the entire address of the individual or firm you are mentioning must be communicated 2 spaces above the greeting and 2 spaces underneath the date.

The names of people, businesses, street corners, roads, and so on must be communicated exactly as they are in the source from which you obtained the address. These specifics shouldn't be compromised. Doing so is improper corporate conduct. It is also important to pronounce the address name accurately. If you pronounce her or his name wrong, she or he might think you do not care about her or him.

There are different dispatch sections in numerous businesses. What you type as the inner address in this part will be replicated on the card. Your letter might not get to its intended recipient if you failed to correctly include the inner address.

5. *Attention line*: A letter that is sent to a corporation or company may occasionally be designated to a specific official

in that organisation to guarantee rapid attention. An attention line should be added to 2 spaces underneath the inner address and 2 spaces over the greeting to accomplish this.

6. *Salutation*: It is a crucial component of a letter, similar to how you embrace someone when you first meet them. It is positioned 2 spaces underneath the attention line or 2 spaces underneath the inner address if there isn't one.

The interior address's company and the composer and viewer's interpersonal connection influence the salutation option.

Use 'Dear Sirs' when writing to a business, corporation, panel, society, club or government body. Constantly keep in mind that the salutation is unaffected by the attention line. Dear Sir or Dear Ma'am would be used as the salutation if you are writing a letter to an official by name.

7. Subject: The goal of the subject section is to make it clear to the viewer what the letter is concerning. It reduces effort in the same way that focuses and referencing sections do. The convention is to compose this sentence with a double space separating it and the greeting and the initial sentence of the letter's body.

Nevertheless, other businesses choose to place the subject section before the greeting and after the attention line.

8. *Body*: The primary goal of a letter seems to be to communicate content, and the primary goal of the statement is to elicit the desired reaction from the audience. Mostly via the letter's body, this is accomplished. As a result, it is crucial to arrange and display the information appropriately.

Reference to any prior communication must be made in the initial paragraph, and the primary point must be presented in the next.

One should make it obvious in the concluding paragraph whatever activity you are counting on the viewer to perform. Alternatively, you can close the letter by outlining your hopes, desires or goals.

Until the letter seems quite lengthy and covers several significant topics, no headers are used for the paragraphs.

9. A complimentary conclusion is a polite approach to taking a break from absence when concluding a letter. It is written 2 spaces underneath the final sentence of the letter's body. The salutation needs to be in harmony with the complimentary conclusion.

10. *Signed name*: The author's name appears as the signature. The complementing closure is positioned over it. A signature can be printed with room to spare 4 spaces underneath the concluding sentence, where the writer's name is often placed.

11. *Typist recognition markings*: Located 1 or 2 spaces underneath the signature, these markings are placed on the left side of the margin of the letter to indicate the letter's writer. The investigator's initials are often placed foremost on letters that are addressed to her or him.

For instance, if Km. Parul Gupta composed the letter after Sri S.P. Shukla had narrated it.

12. *Attachments*: If the letter has any attachments, they should be listed against the enclosing section, which are entered 2 spaces underneath the recognition markings.

The standard format is to enter the shortened form Encl., alongside which the count of enclosing is given.

13. *Replica distributions*: In certain cases, replicas of a letter must be delivered to recipients in addition to the addressee. In these situations, the identities of these individuals must be put immediately beneath the referencing initials or the enclosing indication, if applicable. The identities of the individuals must be listed either chronologically or in ascending order of significance.

14. *Postscript*: A postscript is indeed a sentence that is added following the letter is finished. A postscript (PS) is a sign that the composer did not adequately organise her or his correspondence or that she or he neglected to mention whatever is crucial in the letter's body. It must ideally be eliminated from the perspective of a successful business.

Range of Layout

1. *Stationery*: White sheets are used since they help the lettering to stand out and facilitate comprehension.

Business letters are often written on paper that is 18 1/2 by 11 inches in size. Additional sizes include 8 × 10, 5 × 10, and 5 and a half × 8 and a half inches.

2. *Typing*: Many business correspondences are typed. There are 2 factors at play. The saving effort by typing also provides the letter with a neat aesthetic. Nevertheless, attention must be paid to how cleanly the characters are typed.

3. *Margins*: Margins enhance the appeal of a letter. In a regular-size letter, there should typically be a 1-inch margin on each side and on the bottom and top.

4. *Envelope*: The envelope size must match the sheet on which the text is composed. When using a screen envelope, the letter must be folded so that the inner address is visible. The bare minimum number of bends ought to be utilised.

Arrangement of a Business Letter's Parts and Layouts

Layout describes the methodical grouping of a business letter's elements for improved comprehension. Business letters can be formatted in a variety of ways, including Block, Altered, Semi-Block, Suspended Indention and Demi-Official. Studying the letter's more popular formats will be sufficient, which are as follows:

- For business letters, the complete block format is frequently employed. All the elements are placed closer to the left side of the margin in this arrangement. The paragraphs are spaced using a 2-line format. The sender's and recipient's credentials are written using accessible punctuation, which indicates that commas are omitted from this part of the sentence. Additionally, there are zero commas following the complementing closing. This makes the letter look tidy and uncomplicated. With all the parts pushed to the left side of the margin, it is an easy form to type on. Nevertheless, certain individuals consider it unbalanced because of this.
- *Modified Block*: It is a layout that is used frequently in contemporary Indian business writing. To break up the monotonous effect of the Complete Block Format,

it changes it. The dates and the complements are moved to the right-hand side of the margin, moving 2 of the elements. Other characteristics resemble those of the whole block form.

- *Semi-Block*: This is how letters are often written. To make the letter seem fair, the area is separated equally. At the front core of the sheet, the user's contact is placed, followed by the date, the inner address, the greeting and the compliment information. The sections start 5 spaces after the left side of the margin, whereas the subject sentence is placed closer to the margin.
- Using a hanging indention format is like using a block design, with the exception that all subsequent sentences in every paragraph should be separated by 4 or 5 spaces. Its distinctive look might draw attention fast, yet this feature could also work against it. By drawing the viewer's interest to the letter's appearance instead of its content, it can divert her or him. In the business sector, this fashion was not well liked.
- The biggest current attempt in layout design is the NOMA shape. The National Office Managing Association of America endorses it (NOMA). Additionally recognised there is in the UK. Most of the attributes of the complete block format are present. The left side of the margin as well as the block style's inner address is where each line starts. This form's unique characteristics are:
  - (i) There is neither an answer nor a complimentary conclusion.
  - (ii) Three lines underneath the inner address, in uppercase letters, is the subject line.
  - (iii) Listing elements with numbers start at the left side of the margin; otherwise, the elements are indented five spaces. Entries do not terminate with a full stop.
  - (iv) Underneath the place for a sign, the narrator's identity and position are placed in all capital letters.
  - (v) The composer's initials need to be in the bottom left corner.

C's of International Business Letter Composing: Guidelines

The most common type of business correspondence is business letters, which can be written physically (physical or hard copy) or electronically (soft copy). Business letters are prepared for a variety of purposes, including asking and responding to questions, managing complaints, managing consumer connections, marketing items, asking for credits, gathering payments and gaining the client's goodwill. The letter should guarantee that the required activity is taken and that the intended response is received. As a result, the writer should carefully consider the letter's content.

A letter writer should be familiar with the protocol and regulations of the company they are writing to, as well as the terminology used in formal communication. While composing the letter, the writer should also practice being concise and exact and using a genuine attitude. Two aspects of letter preparation are involved:

- Content planning or deciding what the transmitter intends to say to the recipient.
- Expression planning or the manner of the content includes vocabulary, language selection, tone, and so on.

The author of the letter should place it in the appropriate setting. The accompanying guidelines or requirements for composing business letters often alluded to as the 'business letter composing Cs' must be taken into consideration.

1. *Completion*: An official letter should be comprehensive. There cannot be any facts omitted. All of the recipient's queries that come to mind should be addressed. Consider the letter as follows:

When essential information, such as the insurance number, kind of insurance, title, when the insurance first went into effect, and others, are omitted from the letter, it results in delaying the recipient's ability to take action. Writing credit numbers, user ID numbers, the PNR code, the date the seat was purchased, the travel date, and other pertinent information is required when managing contact with an institution or a ticket inquiry, for instance. The writer needs to make a distinct table of each of the pertinent elements while composing the statement. Furthermore, she or he must make sure that the statement's body contains them. She or he must ascertain whether her or his letter fully addresses all the queries that the recipient is expected to have.

2. The next rule of business statement composing is correctness. The author must initially check that the information is accurate. She or he needs to confirm the data and details. Before recording the facts on paper, she or he must confirm them. Secondly, she or he must be flawless in the adherence to the rules of letter composing. Lastly, she or he needs to proofread the content for typos, grammatical flaws, duplicates that aren't essential and punctuation faults. Concise forms and telegraphic composing, which ought to be ignored when composing a letter, have been introduced by SMS and E-writing.

Improper details, improper claims and unsuitable manner not only leave a negative impact on the listener, but also damage the image and integrity of the firm one is speaking on behalf of.

3. *Clarity*: Business communications should be understandable upon initial reading.

The presenter should try to foresee what the recipient would desire to learn and should convey her or his statement in a style that the recipient can easily understand. The letter's goal and the user's motivations for delivering it should be made clear. To prevent conflict or confusion, the language should be straightforward, and the information should be self-explanatory.

The letter's intended message is ruined by prolonged, convoluted phrases, poor word selection and an aggressive demeanour. Clarity may be added to any communication by picking the intended audience, utilizing concise phrases and properly selecting the terms.

4. *Clarity*: The letter creator needs to be succinct. The goal should be to communicate more with fewer terms. The presenter should rewrite the initial text by switching out low-information terms for high-content terms and tightening up loose constructs. For instance, to provide our cherished consumers with the finest service feasible, I am authorised to provide this proposal while bearing your interests in mind.

We are providing this to our cherished clients with their finest intentions in view, to restate this. The presenter should refrain from being wordy and repetitious; unclear statements and terms should be swapped out for clear ones; using one term rather than 2 would promote brevity. Education can help you develop brevity.

5. *Regard and Courtesy*: Companies want to build connections based on respect and courtesy, and this may be done via a human connection. The communicator might build a personal connection with the reader by stressing the nice and the beneficial and concentrating on you rather than me or us. Being polite has a high return on investment.

The letter should be written in a compassionate and polite tone throughout. If the circumstances call for it, it may change and turn hostile or demanding. Yet it's preferable to refrain from being harsh or offensive.

Courtesy: By communicating with someone politely, one gains their regard. A polite tone shows the sender's kindness and encourages a good reaction from the recipient. Additionally, it promotes a positive perception of the sender's person or business. One should develop tact, consideration and appreciation. The letter must use respectful, cordial language.

How the Business Letter Should Look?

Choosing the right visual effect is nearly as crucial as preparing the content itself. . A well-written letter loses its impact if it is poorly delivered. When writing a letter, the composer cannot stand to ignore the accompanying issues:

a. Quality stationery
b. Appropriate division of space among the parts of a business letter
c. Tidy look and appropriate format
d. Typed, if at all practicable
e. If handwritten, legible and adhering to all fundamental writing conventions.
f. Use grammar, spelling and punctuation correctly

g. Clear foolscap sheet
h. Suitable font (if computer-based)
i. Cleanly and suitably folded sheet
j. Suitable envelope completes the list, and
k. Properly addressed, ideally in the middle of the envelope

To sum up, the objective is to improve global business letter writing by updating communication practices for effective interaction with external entities. In today's global village, business letters serve as lasting records and regulatory documents. They play various roles, including reference, global expansion, regulatory record and goodwill building. Different types, such as official letters, demi-official notes and form letters, cater to diverse needs. Elements like heading, date, reference, internal address, attention line, salutation, subject, body, complimentary conclusion, signed name, and more follow a structured layout. The range of layout considerations includes stationery quality, proper spacing, a tidy appearance, and correctness in typing or legibility in handwritten letters. Adhering to business letter guidelines of the three Cs is crucial. The visual impact, encompassing stationery, spacing, format, typing or handwriting conventions, grammar, folding and addressing, is as vital as the content itself.

Activity

1. What is the chief purpose of incorporating business letters in global communication?
2. How does the format of a business letter differ from that of a personal letter?
3. Explain the significance of the subject line in a business letter.
4. Why is brevity important in business communication?
5. Explore the role of cultural sensitivity in international business letter writing.
6. What is the purpose of the Complete Block format in business letters?
7. How does the signature contribute to the formality and authenticity of business letters?

8. Why is it crucial to select a suitable envelope for a business letter?
9. When is it appropriate to include a postscript, and how does it affect the reader's perception?
10. Explain the purpose and significance of including attachments in a business letter.

13

E-mail Etiquette and Report Writing Globally

E-mail

Through the system of telecommunication and computer connections, customers can receive and send information using electronic mail or e-mail, which is an integral part of the global network of electronic communication. The message could be composed of brief remarks and congratulations, lengthy text documents with visuals and photographs, video recordings or sound, or just plain content. E-mail is an electronic post office because of this, even without a receiver on the other side, it enables communication. It entails that one can deliver e-mails whenever the user wishes and at any moment. The recipient of the text may read it anytime he or she chooses. As a result, for that specific communication, the transmitter and the recipient do not need to interact at the same moment.

Etiquettes of E-mail

1. Quick replies to e-mail communications.
2. For the ease of the recipient, an e-mail should have a subject line.
3. Use succinct words to capture the reader's interest.
4. Minimise rambling and be comprehensive and succinct.
5. Make use of capital and lowercase characters. It's simpler to read. Prevent 'Shouting', which is written in all capital characters.
6. Steer clear of offensive and harsh language.
7. Don't overload your communication with files.

8. If the e-mail platform permits it, constantly include the name. One's address that includes one's name represents a person more accurately than their e-mail address does.
9. Before submitting the e-mail, go over it again and proofread it.
10. Make sure the e-mail is clear of grammar errors and employ spell check to verify proper spelling.

E-mail Benefits

1. It makes it possible to transmit and receive messages from people who have e-mail addresses.
2. It quickly sends the message. It moves quite quickly as a result.
3. It isn't necessary for the recipient of the communication to be there on the other side. The recipient can examine the information by accessing the mailbox at any moment to see if it has been delivered.
4. It is delivered immediately to the recipient's e-mail.
5. It guarantees a better level of information secrecy.
6. It is an incredibly inexpensive form of communication. E-mail can frequently take the place of written correspondence like letters and memos.
7. Since messages can be transmitted at any moment, daytime or nighttime, the time zone factor is less of an issue.
8. Multiple recipients can receive the same message at once.

Report Writing

An organised display of facts about an incident, a course of activity or a particular commercial operation is known as a report. It is a textual record of outcomes, developments, traits, circumstances, developments or the evaluation of documents. An essential administrative resource for formulating decisions is a report. A report conveys facts from a source to a recipient who requires it.

An oral report seems straightforward and simple to deliver. It might involve sharing an opinion or an insight. However, a written report is usually preferable since

1. A report given orally may be rejected at any moment. However, a report in writing is a lasting record.
2. Oral reports frequently lack specificity. The writer strives to be exact when writing a report.
3. A report that is written could be consulted again.
4. There is less transmission-related distortion.

Different Forms Of Global Business Reports

(A) According to the requirements of the law

1. *Informal reports*: These are composed in the style of letters that are sent from one individual to the other. Informal reports often don't adhere to any established format or process. There is no set order among them. As per the firm's comfort and needs, they are constructed. These analyses could be instructive or directional.

2. *Official reports*: A formal report includes one that is created in a predetermined format and delivered to a certain authority in line with predetermined steps.

- *Statutory*: A report is referred to as a statutory report when it is written in the format and guidelines established by law.
- *Non-statutory*: It is a formal report that is generated to assist the administration in formulating policy or making other crucial decisions yet is not mandated by any legislation.

(B) A report could be classified as regular or special depending on how frequently it is released.

1. *Regular or usual reports*: They are created and delivered in regular, predetermined schedules as a part of business globally as usual. They might be sent every day. Bank branch managers often report to the main office on the volume of business done within a specific period.

2. *Special reports*: These focus on a specific event or circumstance. Special reports include topics like whether it would be a good idea to establish a fresh branch or whether there is employee unrest in a specific branch. Special reports cover issues that don't come up often.

(C) A report may be educational depending on its role. A report is informative if it only provides information that is relevant to a problem or circumstance.

On the contrary, it might be categorised as analytic, interpreting or exploratory if it examines the data, draws conclusions and makes recommendations.

(D) We could conduct a discussion about the topic being discussed based on its character.

- Report that identifies the issue
- Report on a fact-finding
- Report on performance
- Technical report and so on.

(E) Depending on how many people are keen on participating in the report-writing process, we could have:

- Individual reports
- Reports from panels or subpanels

Qualities of the Report

An effective report should be

- Succinct and accurate,
- Accurate,
- Clear,
- Relevant and
- Reader-focused

Purpose of the Report

1. It provides the administration with facts.
2. It keeps track of information and polls or research findings for subsequent use.
3. It offers essential facts to the general public, lenders, consumers and investors.
4. It offers suggestions for application in the future.

Report Writing: Key Principles

1. The report must be directed to a specific person or group, such as the Chief Executive or the Board of Directors.
2. It must have a brief, distinct title that makes it obvious what the report is about.
3. The report must include the word of reference so that it becomes evident why it is necessary, as reports are typically written on the demand or advice of a recipient.
4. The content of the report must be organised, logically sequenced and should have headings.
5. Any suggestions must be indicated to draw emphasis to them right away. The official in charge of it might endorse it, and the date must be included.

Preparation of a Report

The 5 phases listed as under should be included when writing a report.

- Looking into the information's sources;
- Taking records;
- Examining the facts;
- Creating an overview; and
- Composing a report

Structure of the Report

(1) *Letter format*: Letter format is advised for informal reports. The header or topic, date, location, greeting, body, complementing closure and sign make up the bulk of the document.

The letter's core is subsequently separated into:

(i) *Introduction*: It describes the scope of the research and the criteria of reference. (It mentions the issue with the word of reference plus pertinent facts.)

(ii) *Outcomes*: The trial's conclusions are discussed.

(iii) The recommendation makes sense in light of the conclusions in the final paragraph of the section.

(2) *Memorandum*: It is more straightforward than a formal letter. At the very top, the date is stated. The identity of the individual to whom the report is written, the identity of the author and the report's content are then listed. The content itself and the conclusion follow thereafter. Similar to a letter, a report's content is broken up into sections with headings and subheadings.

(3) *The letter-text combo format*: The letter-textual mixture format is typically used for lengthy reports. A full report in this format is broken down into 3 main sections: -

(i) Introduction sections

- Letter of presentation or transmission

A letter of transmission is a standard letter used to provide a report from its author to its recipient. It offers everlasting documentation of the transference, displays the date when the report was filed, including the name and title of the presenter, authorises the report, and invites reader feedback. The report's focus mentions the author's informational sources and emphasises unique aspects.

- Cover

In essence, it offers the report a tidy look and safeguards the content against destruction. The name and address of the corporation are printed on some companies' cover pages, which are produced in printed form. Other than that, it includes the study's title, date, number and classification—such as confidential, highly classified, and so on.

- Title

The title page includes the report's topic, the writer's name, the name of the authorities for whom the report was produced, the month and year it was completed, and other information.

- Preface

The majority of the detail regarding the report's features is contained in the opening, which also occasionally mentions the report's shortcomings. Before presenting a report to the viewers, it contains prefatory statements.

- Acknowledgement

Make sure to accurately list the names of the people and companies who assisted in preparing the report, except if you have already done so elsewhere. In doing so, we speak and act with sincerity and courtesy.

- Table of contents

The table makes it clear what distinct items you should include in the report and where they might be referenced or clarified. It is recommended that the relevant page number come after the information.

- List of figures/tables

A thorough and methodically created report might include illustrations, a list of charts, images or diagrams, along with the page number where each might well also be found.

- Abstract or synopsis

The viewer can quickly understand the report's main points—thanks to the synopsis. The report is summarised in an abstract. In actuality, the abstract clarifies the purpose of the report and its importance. In contrast, a summary is a condensed version of the complete report. A summary is longer compared to an abstract.

(ii) The Report's body

- Introduction

An introduction of a report serves to convey the topic to the audience.

- Background information, both historical and technological.
- How the information is organised.
- The study's scope, including its qualifications and restrictions.
- Approval of the reference terms and report.
- Special terminology and symbol descriptions, if there are any.

The purpose and theme of the report must be clearly stated, and there must be sufficient background information to explain to the viewer why the issue was deemed important enough to investigate.

- Methodology

Each report that does not identify where and how the information was gathered is not regarded to be acceptable. There are 2 types of data: and secondary. Material that is employed for the initial time by the author is considered primary, whereas data that has already been employed elsewhere is considered secondary.

- Analysis or Discussion

The report's major portion or part is pertaining to analysis or discussion. Interpretation, analysis and assessment are all included in this section. Using sections and subsections, it carefully describes the several facets of the problem. This section's primary goal is to organise the presentation of data, evaluate its importance, and outline its investigation and any subsequent findings. It has graphs, statistics, charts and more.

- Outcomes

This section includes a presentation of the anticipated outcome of the inquiry, along with a discussion of each component's benefits and drawbacks. Each approach has an in-depth justification. Outcomes are organised and displayed in a logical or sequential order. It might contain images, charts, graphs, tables, infographics, and so forth depending on the section.

- Conclusions

The study essentially concluded at this point, therefore it's important to properly describe the important findings. Nothing additional must be added at this point; all findings should be validated by the prior work. If they are numerous, they can be listed in descending order of significance.

- Suggestions

The conclusion and suggestion ought to be included in the same part if the report is brief since they are interconnected. However, in lengthy reports, this method causes uncertainty in the viewer's thinking and renders it challenging for the author to clarify. The suggestion recommends a plan of action to be followed and details the outcomes. It ought to be expressly stated in the end and serve as the basis for decision making.

(iii) Final Matters

- References/Bibliography

By describing them at the closing of the report, the researcher gives acknowledgment to the relevant contributor in this area. When there are few references, they are listed at the bottom of the following section where they are utilised as footnotes. Additionally, if there are several of them, a distinct document should be attached.

- Glossary

A description of each technological term in the report's glossary is provided. Furthermore, as with the list of references, if there are few references, annotations are added; however, if there are enough, a distinct glossary part is included.

- Appendices

It includes graphs, charts and analytical tables that are necessary to complement the report's primary body. However, such information can be securely omitted by the viewer without affecting their comprehension of the report's facts. Additionally, the appendices must contain the confirming or relevant proof and papers if the reader wants to review them in depth.

To conclude, e-mail communication plays a pivotal role in worldwide communication, showcasing its adaptability in transmitting diverse information forms asynchronously. Adhering to e-mail etiquette involves highlighting the significance of prompt responses, well-defined subject lines, succinct language and other courteous practices. The advantages of e-mail encompass prompt delivery, confidentiality, cost-effectiveness and global accessibility. Furthermore, written reports are significant over oral presentations that accentuate their lasting documentation and clarity. The various types of business reports underscore the importance of customised communication within professional settings.

Activity

1. Describe the elements of an e-mail message.
2. How can the efficiency of an e-mail be improved through the use of concise language?
3. How does e-mail ensure a better level of information secrecy?
4. How does e-mail handle the time zone factor?
5. List some qualities of an effective report.
6. What is the importance of a list of figures or tables in a report?
7. How can visual elements like charts and graphs enhance the effectiveness and clarity of a report?
8. Explain the role of a cover page in a report.
9. What are the five stages involved in the development of a report?
10. What should be included in the conclusions section of a report?

14

Legal and Ethical Considerations in International Business Writing

Significance of Ethics and Legal Role

Building customer trust is based on protection, security and privacy. Customers depend on the image and identity of business initiatives to establish a trustworthy business connection. Confidence disappears when workers act immorally, illegally or unethically. It is frequently hard to get back.

Among the top credit reporting companies, Equifax, experienced a hack in September 2017, which exposed the personal data of about 147 million customers worldwide. Managers at Equifax were aware that the business's hardware and software were open to hacking, according to findings from studies conducted by the Federal Trade Commission and congressional supervision panels. They hadn't put in place the fundamental security procedures and guidelines to prevent this kind of intrusion. As a component of an international settlement, the business was required to compensate up to $425 million for its unethical conduct. The Federal Trade Commission has allowed people to file asserts against Equifax until 2024, so the consequences of the data leak are expected to take a long time to go away.

Ethical and Legal Writing

The personal and professional norms of conduct that you uphold make up your ethics and legal aspects. It determines the standards of integrity, compassion, dependability and other qualities that characterise your actions and public persona.

Ethics establishes standards for your interactions with other people. Generally speaking, ethical behaviour is seen as voluntary and individual—often determined by your personal beliefs about what is acceptable and unacceptable. Every worker in a company has the option to act morally or immorally. You are having a philosophical conversation with yourself every time you consider the conduct you value in your professional and personal lives. This dialogue helps you to define the norms for conduct you want to maintain.

Ethical Consideration for Legal Role

Ethical reasoning frequently captures the shifts in awareness that society and individuals experience and is more topical. Amendments to laws are frequently preceded and facilitated by ethical thinking.

Certain professions have established codes of ethics, including engineering, reporting and healthcare. A rule of ethics consists of a promise to handle customers, consumers, staff members and other people connected to a profession honestly and ethically. For instance, the majority of medical practitioners today agree that doctors, nurses and other experts in the field should constantly uphold the Hippocratic Oath. The origin of this duty can be traced back to Hippocrates, the Greek doctor of antiquity.

Involuntary duty refers to the initiatives that community members would like to see business workers engage in to better their neighbourhoods. Community building initiatives or assistance at a nearby food bank are two instances.

The Phronesis (or Practical Wisdom) Idea

We can act morally when we possess phron sis, pronounced fro-NEE-sis. The Japanese business scholar Ikujiro Nonaka and Harvard Business School instructor of administration Hirotaka Takeuchi (2011) address the differences between the concept and usage of ethics and the qualities of an effective leader in their paper "The Big Concept: The Wise Leader", which appears in the Harvard Business Evaluation and addresses administration and ethical choices. According to the researchers' conclusion, CEOs need to lead with morality and ethics to integrate practical knowledge.

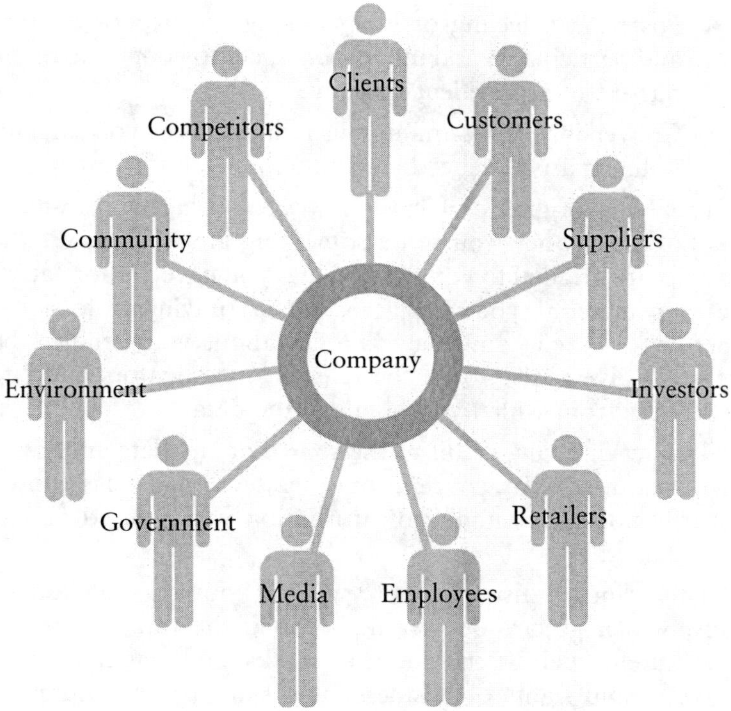

Figure 14.1: Legal and Ethical Considerations in International Business Writing
Source: https://human.libretexts.org/Courses/Harrisburg_Area_Community_College/Business_Writing_for_Everyday_Use/01%3A_New_Page/1.04%3A_Ethical_Considerations_in_Business_Writing

From the standpoint of business writing, proficient writers share useful information by:

- Giving clarifications and specifics
- Adding details that are relevant to the subject
- Evaluating content to ascertain its effectiveness
- Introducing, summarizing and transitioning
- Examining material to imagine the effects of potential decisions or reactions
- Including data that takes stakeholder worries and feedback into account
- Creating material that is simple for readers to comprehend

- Fostering a feeling of unity among the paper's viewers and participants and motivating them to cooperate in the pursuit of a prevalent objective
- Conversing with as numerous individuals as you can and utilizing an audience-based communication strategy

Falsifying origins or facts is known as plagiarism, and it usually occurs when you write something and then assert the concepts are original to you. Ensure that you have authorization to use any materials you come across when studying professional paperwork. When composing content about your studies, be certain to give praise to all the relevant investigators and cite the sources from which you obtained the data.

The act of giving credit to the source of any data employed in written form, ideas, concepts or other developments is known as attribution. The validity of attribution varies based on the development.

This principle also applies to what is known as intellectual assets, which go beyond writing. Among the things that fall under intellectual assets are trademarks and patents (these are ownership rights of business labels), logos, procedures or catchphrases. None of these items may be utilised without the correct acknowledgment or consent of the relevant organisation or person.

A business employs to demonstrate that a product has been filed with the US Patent and Trademark Office or has been trademarked. One illustration might involve Nike and their well-known swoosh logo.

When writing in an expert setting, the legal ramifications are particularly noteworthy. While plagiarism in a classroom may outcome in a failing grade, it can also land you a job at a company which can lead to costly legal action and potentially even time in prison. Respecting these guidelines is not only morally right but also required by law. To avoid misleading the reader, ensure that all sources are appropriately cited.

Take a few moments to look over the subsequent web pages to learn more about registered trademarks, copyrights and trademarks: The United States Office of Patents and Trademarks

Books, movies and software that are legally safeguarded from distribution are included in the scope of the copyright legislation. The sign for copyright is represented by a ©. Plagiarism and copyright vary in that the former is a legal matter. The exclusive right to reproduce a copyrighted work rests with the individual or entity that owns it.

Ethics and legal roles are crucial in business, impacting customer trust and global incidents like the Equifax hack. Ethical writing shapes personal and professional conduct, emphasizing the voluntary nature of ethical behaviour. Considerations for legal roles influence societal awareness and guide legal amendments. Professions like engineering and healthcare adhere to ethical codes, ensuring honest treatment of stakeholders. The concept of *phron sis* or practical wisdom in ethical leadership emphasises the need for CEOs to lead with morality and ethics for practical knowledge integration.

Activity

1. In what ways can ethical considerations influence alterations in laws and regulations within a society?
2. In what ways does the image and identity of a business play a role in creating a dependable connection with customers?
3. How can businesses balance ethical considerations with legal obligations in international business writing?
4. What is the significance of the Hippocratic Oath in the medical profession and how does it relate to ethical considerations?
5. Explain the role of practical wisdom in introducing, summarizing and transitioning in business writing.
6. What is phronēsis and how does it contribute to acting morally in business leadership?

Part VI

Oral Communication Skills for Global Business

15
Techniques for Effective International Presentation

Presentation

A presentation represents a serious subject. Its goal is to give a viewpoint or enlighten, clarify, and convince the listener. It might present a commodity, clarify a procedure or recount an encounter. At a lecture, workshop or corporate event, it is presented to a limited, educated group. The audience then has the opportunity to ask queries.

With formal education and experience, presentation skills could be built and nurtured. As with giving a speech, preparation must be completed in 4 phases:

1. Learning about the setting, or you can state the various presenting aspects, and where the presentation will be made.
2. Creating the content and necessary graphics.
3. Taking good care of one's looks and manners.
4. Test out your presenting approach.

Essential Factors of International Presentation

1. *The location*: One would feel more at ease if one is acquainted with the area. However, don't neglect to inspect the space and all necessary materials a few minutes ahead of the presentation. One should attempt to become acquainted with the venue, the seating layout and the speaker's posture if it is outdoors. Examine the visual aids in detail. Take note of its location and projections.

2. *The coordinator*: Do your best to learn as much as you can regarding the organiser, the firm's name and the names of its key personnel.

3. *The context*: You must be aware of the context where you will be giving your presentation, such as a corporate conference, workshop or lecture.

4. Check the amount of period you have accessible in advance. One must adhere strictly to the time limit.

5. *Extra speakers*: Determine the other speakers. Will there be people representing competitor companies? What role does their company hold? Regardless of whether they are there, be cautious not to say anything negative about opponents.

6. *The viewer*: The presentation should take the viewer's demands and inclinations into consideration. The viewer's characteristics will determine the speech's topic and tone. Be careful with the terminology you employ in the presentation; avoid making any potentially offensive references. Among the elements to consider is the viewer's age range. The following pointers offer useful tips:

(a) Kids enjoy hearing tales and are drawn to dramatic performances.

(b) University and high school learners prefer to be considered adults. They are receptive to fresh concepts, and value an honest, clear perspective yet are also inclined to be analytical, and they anticipate a well-prepared speech with relevant information.

(c) Younger adults have the most sophisticated demographic; they have a diverse spectrum of interests and a forward-thinking outlook. They enjoy novel initiatives and concepts yet are also quite critical.

(d) The middle-aged population is conservative and is less likely to readily embrace fresh concepts. Individuals possess significant life expertise and understanding yet might not be as excited regarding modifications or fresh concepts. They hear with attention yet are not as quick to adopt.

(e) The majority of the time, senior adults are curious about current events and fresh developments. They also enjoy being brought back to the past. What level of education and income does the population have? Whatever generation group's extremely educated viewers are particularly critical. As a group, the wealthy are opposed to societal reform.

International Presentation Design

For each minute you discuss, you require an hour of preparation. The most crucial step is to choose your words carefully, gather the necessary data and provide them with a suitable structure. It should be coherent and possess a clear progression from one idea to the next one. Include the location, the introduction and the closing words in your notes for the entire presentation. After that, refine, revise and perfect it until you have a strong presentation that fits the time allotted.

- *Length*: The session moves along at an approximate rate of 100 words per minute. Give a speech to determine your speaking pace. A 2-minute speech can be composed on an A4 size page with 1 and a half spacing line and 12 font size. 400–500 words make up a presentation that lasts 4-5 minutes.
- A speech should sound conversational. Employ simple lines so the audience may understand. Make sure the language you employ is appropriate for your viewers. Be formal in your approach. Communicating in a formal context differs from communicating in a societal or personal context in terms of formality.
- *Humour*: Make sure one can laugh without getting awkward or looking ridiculous. Humour ought to be unforced, carefree, pleasurable and pertinent to the subject. No audience must feel embarrassed or offended by it.

International Presentation Outline Preparation

An agenda for a presentation serves a similar purpose as one for a textual report: it assists you in structuring your content to have the most possible influence on your listeners. Develop your blueprint in steps to achieve efficient establishment:

- *Describe your core concept and intent*: Make periodic checks as you create your outline to ensure that the topics, structure, linkages and title are relevant to your goal and key concept.
- *Arrange your main ideas and supporting details*: To maintain the pace of the one main notion you wish to

communicate in each significant statement, describe each of them as a full sentence. Furthermore, ensure the ideas are presented in a logical and efficient sequence by paying attention to the sequence.

- *Determine your opening, middle and conclusion*: Beginning using the body, assign a rank to every significant point and subpoint based on its position in your design. Then list the key elements for your opening and closing.
- Display your contacts. The changes you intend to utilise to go from one section to the following should be written out in whole sentences. In the speech's content, don't forget to use more transitions between key topics.
- *Indicate your resource*: When creating your bibliography, ensure it is clear to read, adheres to a standard structure and contains all the information required to distinguish your numerous resources. Be ready to cite important resources during your discussion as necessary.
- *Select a title:* Not every presentation or talk has a title. A headline, nevertheless, can be helpful if somebody else will deliver your work or market it beforehand.
- *Reduce points and changes to a few crucial utterances*: Pick words that would help you recall the details of every point so you could communicate clearly. Additionally, you might wish to use whole lines to move between key topics or at important parts of your opening or conclusion.
- *Including delivery and cues*: Make a note of the locations in the design during practice when you intend to halt for highlights, talk more gradually, utilise a visual, and so on.

Visual Tools

They are used by the presenter to convey information in a structured manner, demonstrate points using diagrams and display data. The viewers can view a graphic overview of the topics and receive visual reinforcement for whatever they have heard. Either one or multiple of the accompanying sophisticated visual tools are appropriate:

1. You can put up posters in practically any place. Despite

being outdated, advertising professionals who travel to rural communities have discovered this to be a fairly reliable strategy.

2. A flip chart needs support or an easel. The most effective application is interactive displays. One can display thoughts from the crowd on it. Then concentrate on it while the people are present. The audience members enjoyed seeing their suggestions recorded during the lecture.
3. Overhead projectors (OHP) are highly common and widely accessible. Use high-quality transparency for making slides. Insert no more than six lines on a slide. Make your writing or typing legible to the entire audience.
4. If accessible, PPT projection can indeed be employed. Don't complicate the slides. Steer clear of motion or colour. Audio should not be used to animate the slides. The presentation should make good use of visuals. Properly design them to highlight a topic with an illustration, list the essential elements or show a graph or diagram. Studies show that 60% of people prefer to see some visuals on slides and the remaining 40% feel that visuals are an absolute must in presentations.

Guidelines for the Successful International Presentation

A presenter must be aware of their physical language, paralanguage, presentation skills, timing and other factors for better presentation to make oral communication.

Listening Effectively

Understanding oral communication requires the recipient to concentrate. It is the audience's job to pay attention and attempt to comprehend the presenter, just as the presenter possesses a role to try to be comprehended. Listening is perhaps the biggest crucial communication ability of everyone. You have a bigger obligation to hear the higher in the organisation you are in.

Johnson: The capability to comprehend spoken communication and react appropriately.

M.V. Rodriques: Obtaining, interpreting and responding to the signal obtained from the transmitter are all parts of the listening procedure.

Mr. Leland Brown: It is possible to activate and deactivate listening both intentionally and involuntarily. It begins with the recipient growing conscious of the need to pay attention and attend to what is been stated.

Process of Listening

Phase one: At this point, the audience did little more than focus on the presenter to understand the speech. You will know you have absorbed the narrator's speech if you can repeat their statements.

Phase two: This is dependent on the vocabulary, expertise, perspective and other factors of the audience. The information is misconstrued if the audience does not appropriately perceive the terms.

Phase three: At this point, the audience chooses how to use the knowledge that has been provided.

You might decide whether to embrace what you perceive whenever you are attending a business speech. The decision you adopt at this point in the review phase is essential to the process of listening.

Phase four: The audience's reaction to the content can be expressed verbally or nonverbally. The reply informs the presenter of the audience's understanding of the content and her or his reaction.

Benefits

1. Understanding the organisation is aided by listening.
2. Listening to others can lead to improved policy decisions.
3. Listening soothes the irate workers.
4. Listening is crucial to the achievement of the open-door regulation.
5. Listening makes it easier to identify potential hazardous regions before they grow touchy.

Steps for Listening Effectively

1. *Eye contact*: If a listener does not fix her or his gaze on the presenter, she or he is not keen on hearing what is being said. Eye contact is a skill that a listener should display. It gives motivation to the presenter.
2. *Physical displays of interest*: A listener should demonstrate that sh/e is involved in what is being spoken. Nonverbal cues like suitable facial gestures, eye contact and positive head movements could be employed to transmit meaning to the presenter.
3. *Refrain from performing any diverting motions or activities*: This includes checking one's wristwatch, shuffling documents, fiddling with pencils, reading newspapers or correspondence, and similar diverting tasks.
4. *Pose queries*: A good listener constantly checks their comprehension by asking queries to clarify any ambiguities. The presenter becomes aware that sh/e is listening with focus.
5. Assist the presenter in relaxing and being conscious of the eager audience with your approach. Be experienced in listening as well as perceived to listen.
6. Resist interrupting to challenge or fight regarding things, saying things like 'That is not so', 'demonstrate it' and other such phrases. Following the speaker's statement, a skilled listener will comprehend what they heard.
7. *Pay careful attention*: Even if people disagree with the presenter's strategy, you still have a right to be acknowledged.
8. *No favouritism*: It is usually preferable to put aside individual opinions and attitudes regarding a presenter and her or his points of view. This is a bad habit and the presenter occasionally feels uncomfortable as a result.
9. *Pay attention to nonverbal indications*: Look for the major ideas. Keep an eye out for nonverbal indicators that help to express meaning, such as the tone of the voice, body language and others. They can be written down by the audience as they will aid in determining whether the presenter comes across as genuine in her or his opinions.

10. *Steer clear of acting attentive*: Numerous audiences get into the habit of acting attentive. They maintain a fixed gaze on the presenter and make an effort to come across as attentive listeners. They frequently overlook many of the speaker's crucial remarks.

Postures and Appearance during the Presentation

One's physical attributes and character have a significant influence.

1. Wear appropriate attire. Make sure you are properly prepared from head to toe if you are not accustomed to wearing formal attire.
2. Before you begin, remember that the viewers take note of your body language.
3. Be in a comfortable and calm standing posture. Hold your position firmly and inhale deeply.
4. Make a hand-related decision (not in a pocket). It might be helpful to have paper, a deck of cards and a pencil in hand.
5. Let your face relax. It can take some practice.
6. Making eye contact is crucial. In 5 seconds, scan the audience as a whole.

   Do not forget to look everyone in the eye. If you're at ease, grin broadly and greet the day.
7. Talk loud enough to be heard by the people at the back. The listeners become uninterested when a speaker speaks at extremes of volume.
8. The tone and amplitude of the voice must change depending on the subject and content of the talk.
9. Use breaks. Audiences become overburdened if too many statements or concepts are presented.
10. Ensure that your health is in perfect shape. You'll be active, eager and self-assured if your health is strong. Additionally, the throat, tongue and complete communication systems are impacted by one's physical condition and health.

Presentation Rehearsal

1. Newbie presenters should practice giving presentations in person. The performance is primarily to blame for the presentation's accomplishment, regardless of how much work and thought you put into the text's preparation.
2. You can check the style and language during a rehearsal to see whether they are appropriate for conversation. It is in practice sufficient to simply read aloud. The only way to determine if the statements are comfortable and natural in speech is to try to present them to an audience.
3. Continue to practice until you feel confident using the subject in conversation.
4. Testing the timing also benefits from the practice.
5. The textual content will initially be longer than is necessary for the allotted time. You must repeat talking out aloud multiple times if you're just starting.
6. After practicing in front of a mirror, and then in front of any audience that may be gathered to provide constructive criticism, like a small circle of close colleagues or family.
7. Performing a whole costume rehearsal is worthwhile for your comfort.
8. Avoid memorizing speeches because it leads to dependency and can be very confusing if you miss even one word.

During the Presentation

If you can use the following strategies throughout the event, you can leave a positive impression:

- Don't rush the start.
- While you initially enter the room, take a second to place your documents and find a comfortable position. Afterward, stand up straight, take a glance slowly in all directions, create eye contact with a few listeners, customise the microphone (typically, it ought to be placed 4 to 6 cm from the mouth), and begin speaking in a loud yet confident voice.

- Give the first phrase you can remember. By recalling the opening statement, you may make eye contact and start building connections right away. You, therefore, seem more certain and competent as a result of this.

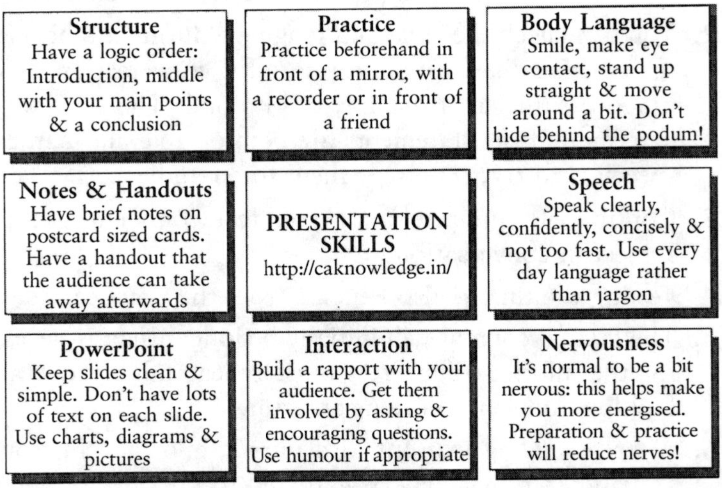

Figure 15.1: Key Points for Effective International Presentation

Source: https://caknowledge.com/effective-presentation-skills/

- When you have begun the talk, be especially cautious to keep eye contact with the listeners during the presentation. Choose numerous individuals from the audience and move your eyes from one to the next. Establishing eye contact will allow you to better evaluate the impression you are making.
- Regulate your tone while talking in front of a listener.
- This implies speaking in normal tones yet loud enough for everybody in the room to hear you. To increase importance, change your tone and talking rate.
- Clearing the throat or coughing regularly is prone to draw the listener's focus away from the presentation and toward the presenter. Prevent these practices that might irritate the listener. Moreover, stay away from irrelevant filler terms and phrases, such as 'Well', 'You know', 'Uh', 'Okay' and similar ones. Silence is preferable to filler

words that have no real purpose. Talk loudly, precisely and with each syllable pronounced properly.

- Speak slowly instead of speaking out of practice. When a presenter speaks quickly, it is challenging for the listener to follow what is being said. To make it easier for people to hear, talk more slowly.
- Occasionally, bodily movements are used to create messages both impressive and intelligible. To avoid employing the arms and hands excessively, attempt to be mindful. By making the correct movements, employ your hands to emphasise any comments. The statements delivered will be livelier if you simultaneously change your facial emotion. To retain and pique listener engagement, employ visual aids. If required, employ a pointer.
- Having the appropriate stance is crucial for conveying the right message. Keep your head high and your hands off the stage.
- The listeners would let you know how you are performing and if you should cut the talk short as you're presenting your message. Pay close attention to any unwanted comments made, such as speaking, giggling, shifting chairs or other signals of displeasure or disapproval.
- The listener receives multiple meanings from clothes. As a result, dress elegantly and deliberately in casual yet professional apparel. Attempt to appear just a little bit nicer than the typical audience member to appreciate them.
- In the case of a lengthy speech, the audience participants are prone to become distracted. Employ jokes to keep the viewer's attention. But if you're not good at telling jokes, don't do it as you might come across as a joke! Jokes should connect to the subject matter of your talk. Never employ jokes that could offend someone because of their ethnicity, gender, race, age or origin.
- Conclusions are highly crucial. A strong conclusion helps to uplift the listener's spirits. A strong presenter would restate their primary points and stress what they want

the listener to accomplish or believe in their closing statements. Once the end is stated, the presenter shouldn't annoy the listeners by continuing to speak for a further five or ten minutes.

After Completing the Presentation

The majority of speeches conclude with discussions with the listeners.

Even if the query and reply session begins after the presentation, one must make it known right away that one is willing to address any inquiries. You won't get distracted, lose your line of thought, or maybe lose out on time because of this preceding statement. One can successfully manage this crucial section of the presentation by using the following methods:

- *Handout Materials*: As soon as the session is over, pass out the materials you had previously made to the listeners.
- *Promote Queries*: If the scenario allows for time for queries and answers, solicit queries from the listeners. Establish a time frame for this discussion.
- *Repeat Queries*: Pay close attention to the query, then say it aloud to yourself and the rest of the listeners to be certain you comprehend it.
- *Request Clarity*: If a query is unclear or ambiguous, ask the asker to clarify it. When responding to the question, keep the entire audience in mind. Give a clear, concise response. To minimise a drawn-out discussion or further queries, maintain your response to be succinct and to the point.
- *Recognise Your Ignorance*: Do not claim to comprehend anything if you do not have the reply to a query. Instead, you openly acknowledge the truth and promise the listener that the solution will be available in a certain amount of time.
- *Treat Politely*: Be courteous to all questioners. Be firm, yet reasonable and polite, regardless of whether the inquiry is hostile.

- *Maintain Control*: Don't let one or two people dominate the query and answer session. Be sure you engage and include all participants. After responding to the final query, wrap up the presentation's key points and express gratitude to the listeners for the chance to speak with them. When the conference is over, take a look around and make eye contact with everyone. Lastly, collect your materials before stepping away from the stage.

International Online Presentation

International online presentations enable one to connect with more individuals in a shorter period, yet they call for certain planning and expertise. One should constantly check with the audience to determine whether they possess any queries because you can't always rely on nonverbal cues to detect listener uncertainty or dissatisfaction.

Observe the following rules:

- Think about providing sample study resources in advance.
- If at all feasible, practice utilizing the device live.
- Keep things as simple as you can in the presentation.
- Request comments often.
- Give everybody a lot of time to interact and become accustomed to the display they are observing.

To summarise, successful international business presentations demand thorough preparation and thoughtful consideration of various components. The primary aim is to compellingly present a perspective or convey information to a limited, knowledgeable audience, allowing for audience inquiries. A combination of presentation skills, formal education and experience contributes significantly to success, involving tasks like understanding the setting, creating content and graphics, ensuring a polished appearance and testing the approach. Key factors for international presentations include awareness of the location, the coordinator, the context, time constraints, other speakers and audience characteristics. Crafting a presentation involves careful word selection, creating coherent and well-organised content, and catering to the audience's preferences. Visual aids are crucial, and effective listening is emphasised for both presenters and audiences. Posture, appearance and rehearsal collectively play a crucial role in a successful presentation, with guidance for during and after the session, along with specific considerations for online presentations.

Activity

1. What are the crucial phases in preparing for a successful international presentation?
2. What factors should be considered for an effective international presentation location?
3. What feedback mechanisms can be used to gather audience input during an online presentation?
4. What are the differences between delivering a presentation in person and online?
5. How can a presenter effectively leverage technology to enhance audience understanding?
6. Why is it important to consider the level of formality in language when communicating internationally?
7. How can a presenter effectively engage an audience with diverse cultural backgrounds?
8. What materials should be handed out to the audience after an international presentation?
9. How can a presenter ensure that humour resonates effectively across various cultural norms?
10. How does the selection of attire impact the perceived professionalism of a speaker in an international setting?
11. What role do cultural nuances play in determining the acceptability of certain presentation styles?

16

Conducting and Participating in Global Meetings

Global Meeting

Active communication is most frequently used in global meetings. At different tiers in any company, it is crucial to facilitate a direct, in-person connection. Between global meeting participants, they act as a means of oral communication. Nevertheless, they are accompanied by textual communication, such as announcements to gather participants, agendas to guide global meetings, minutes to document the events, and reports to relay facts to senior authorities.

A gathering of people to discuss strategies for completing a given task with a deadline is known as a meeting. The group's participants have similar backgrounds, shared issues and shared passions.

The definition of a committee given by W.H. Newman is "A panel of a group of individuals particularly assigned to carry out certain administrative tasks. It demands unfettered communication between its individuals and solely operates as a group".

"A panel is a group of persons who gather by the plan to debate or take a decision about a certain issue", according to Hicks and Gullet's definition of the term. Researchers do not consider groups that happen unexpectedly or spontaneously in the concept of a committee since committee global meetings follow a set agenda.

A meeting is an officially scheduled event when a problem affecting many people is discussed.

Objective

Each of the following goals could be the focus of a meeting:

- To educate and enlighten the individuals on the contents.
- To comprehend the circumstances
- To hear the individuals'opinions
- To allow individuals to share knowledge and suggestions
- To encourage participants to embrace adjustments
- To settle arguments and misunderstandings
- To make decisions regarding issues that will have an impact on the group or company
- To encourage members to be optimistic

Types

(*a*) *Depending on how it works*:

1. *To provide facts*: These gatherings are held to share details and to get the speakers' and members' thoughts on it.

2. *To consult*: To make a good conclusion, the individuals are consulted during consultation global meetings to get their ideas and views.

3. *To carry out ideas*: This kind of a gathering is arranged to collect fresh concepts or recommendations for carrying out a task. Global meetings of this kind are organised when the individuals' collaboration is necessary for the efficient completion of an assignment.

(*b*) *According to the formality*:

1. An organised meeting, such as a parliamentary session, a state assembly, a corporation investor meeting, management-employment talks, an institution senate, or a council or executive body.

2. *Semi-organised global meetings*: These include group meetings, governing councils, general bodies of nonprofit companies, advisory bodies and administration global meetings.

3. Ad-hoc gatherings of workgroups, brainstorming workshops and other forms of unstructured gatherings.

Procedure to Conduct a Meeting

The Latin term for knowledge is where the word 'notice' gets its origin from. The expression when used in regard to a meeting denotes informing the individual in concern about the meeting. Only after giving notice to the parties involved can a meeting be legally conducted. The notice notifies individuals of the meeting's day, time and location, as well as the topic to be addressed and, if feasible, the corresponding contributions anticipated from various meeting attendees.

Agenda

An agenda comprises a collection of subjects that will be discussed during a meeting. A well-structured agenda would aid the Chairperson in steering the meeting's business and guaranteeing that choices are made in a timely way.

A draft of the agenda, as well as the meeting agenda should be distributed to all participants. The agenda elements should be organised in sequential order. The permission of the participants is required if any changes are made to the sequence. Agenda preparation is an extremely beneficial practice:

1. The participants are better able to plan for the meeting when the agenda is distributed beforehand.
2. The agenda's predetermined sequence aids the chairperson in running the meeting efficiently.
3. It guarantees that only topics pertinent to that specific meeting are brought up for discussion.
4. It guarantees that each subject is adequately discussed.
5. It makes creating the minutes easier.

When creating the agenda, keep the following things in mind:

1. It must be precise and explicit.
2. It must be presented in a brief style.
3. The regular things must come first, followed by the more important issues.
4. On the agenda, any items with an identical or related nature must be presented next to one another.

5. Everything on the agenda needs to fall within the parameters of the gathering.
6 . Every item on the agenda should be laid out in the context of the notice summoning the session.

Meeting Minutes

The agenda's elements or themes are addressed in order, each individually throughout the meeting. Each person expresses their comments and thoughts while also debating the advantages and disadvantages of every agenda point. Eventually, they reach certain judgments or decisions that are constantly recorded in official documents. They are known as meeting minutes.

Therefore, minutes are the authoritative recordings of the meeting's activities. In other terms, this is a summary of the conversations that were had and the conclusions that were made during the meeting. It is the responsibility of an authorised individual to explicitly record all such conversations, debates and conclusions in writing.

The objective of taking notes is twofold:

1. To act as an official document of the meeting.
2. To act as a foundation for subsequent conversations.

The meeting minutes should include the following information:

1. The date and the meeting list.
2. A set of the people who witnessed the meeting.
3. A set of people who did not present and for whom sincere apology has been provided.
4. A documentation of the preceding minutes' confirmation and any revisions approved by the group.
5. The vital, essential backdrop to the subject being discussed.
6. A precise and unambiguous documentation of the resolution or conclusion made, as well as, if necessary, the people or institutions in charge of carrying out the required activity.
7. Distinct minutes must be prepared on the ethical problem when the discussion of a particular instance raises one.

Minute Types

1. Resolutions' minutes. Just the resolutions adopted at a conference are noted in the form of minutes, and all conversations that took place before the resolutions are not mentioned.

- Decisions that fall under the purview of the panel are presented with the phrase 'it was concluded that'.
- On occasion, meeting participants lack the authority to decide a particular issue. They are only able to suggest their viewpoint to higher-ups who can make decisions.
- It has been decided that Sri Y. K. Yadav would be selected as the business's deputy manager having reference from August 1, 2008, and would receive monthly compensation of Rs. 40,000 along with additional incentives by corporate policies.
- It has been decided to suggest leaving out clause 7 of the MD's employment agreement because the adjustments must be accepted by her or him.

2. Narrative minutes. A study and narrative minutes have certain similarities. The resolutions adopted here are also listed along with a brief description of the conversation and ballot procedure.

Management of Media

A commercial entity tries to connect with a bigger segment of society through mass communication, which is an aspect of a further level of communication. Both the addressor as well as the recipient is identified in a business letter. The business enterprise is the letter writer, while the recipient is a specific individual, by identity, title, organisation or legal body. In contrast, in mass media, the sender is more ambiguous or unidentified but the letter-writer or presenter is stated. This does not imply that mass media has no intended audience. In actuality, mass communication seeks to connect with a specified target audience that is not bound to any particular location. Because of this, mass media campaigns must ensure that their messages not only reach their intended viewers but also grab their interest. In this stage, it is critical to a company's development that it has a capable media administration division (often referred to as the PR department) to handle all of these media-related tasks.

Press Release

Press releases refer to the declaration of the significant statement or progress that a company wishes to make regarding itself to the general audience, via the media and other channels. A company might use direct, particular or generic communication methods to convey messages. Personal writings, e-mails, pamphlets, reports, telephonic conversations and direct mailings of materials are all examples of direct communications. Press releases, on the other hand, emerge crucial when the information to be delivered is of common significance to a sizable portion of society dispersed across many targeted groups. Any corporate group that desires to share the news with the audience will include in its press releases a variety of events and business-based details that the audience may be keen to learn about. Financial outcomes, product releases, achievements, new branch offices, managerial changes, investor and user advantages, community-focused proposals, joint ventures and tie-ups, business closures, prizes and accomplishments, rankings and evaluations, study discoveries, global meetings and conferences, and so on are typical topics for press releases. Press releases don't result in any financial rewards for either the company that issues them or the media that publishes them. However, if managed correctly, they contribute to improving the company's reputation in the public eye.

Press reports and press releases are two distinct things. A press report is written by a reporter who covers an occurrence independently for a publication or news institution. A corporation issues a press release when it submits content for publication that was created in-house.

Features of an Effective Press Release

1. *It must be newsworthy*: This is the first and most important requirement for an effective press release. Because nobody will be eager to peruse it if it lacked significant news worth, and no publication could accept it for publication.

2. *It must be technically accurate*: Being technically accurate is an issue of authenticity, and authenticity is a key business communication concept. Firms must also be aware that misrepresenting the truth to deceive the audience may result in short-term gains, but it will eventually reverse.
3. It must be succinct and to the point. Newspaper editors rarely have time to edit and trim a long announcement and create proper text, and the room is constantly at a premium. A release will have a better possibility of being incorporated if it is succinct. Press releases intended for local media should be longer than those for nationwide newspapers.
4. It ought to be written in clear, colloquial language because readers lose interest in news that is difficult to comprehend. It's as effective as not viewing it if a reader chooses not to peruse it or to return to it afterward. So, it is important to compose the press release.
5. It is appropriate to be published in the journal or magazine that it is being delivered to. Company announcements, for instance, shouldn't be issued to publications covering sports, movies or literature.
6. Be sure that the pertinent 5Ws have indeed been properly addressed.

Who? Identify the parties engaged. Generally, names are significant.

What? Describe the significant event.

When? Specify the duration. The timeframe of the press statement is crucial as the old stuff is not news.

Where? The location is also crucial.

Why? Even while it might not necessarily be able to explain, if these facts are disclosed, they give the release more substance.

Press releases are frequently fairly brief therefore the author will need to exercise judgment in deciding what information to convey.

In addition to this, there are more considerations that should be made when planning the releases:

- Each release must include a headline that is attractive and enticing yet not deceptive.
- The opener must be intriguing for the initial 1 or 2 paragraphs. They must also give the essence.
- Paragraphs ought to be succinct, and subcategories ought to be used if appropriate.
- A cover letter ought to be sent with each release.

Press Conference

When a company has important information to share with the media and whenever a further thorough strategy and conversation are required than what can be provided by a press release, a press conference (also known as a news briefing or media conference) is arranged.

Two main motives exist for conducting a media conference. One seems to enable a newsmaker who receives numerous inquiries from journalists and responds to each of them instead of fielding numerous phone conversations. Another is to attempt and get media exposure for a subject that previously did not attract reporters.

One or multiple presenters might give a message during a press conference, and then journalists might ask queries. There may be merely questioning on occasion, or there may be a message with no queries allowed. Journalists can ask queries, get responses and quotes, and take pictures at a media conference. It is important to keep the following in mind when planning press conferences:

- A week before the briefing, department editors and journalists must get an invite. A phone conversation can indeed be conducted to notify the journalists of the conference a day or 2 before the scheduled date.
- Plan your media conference for between 9 and 11 in the morning or 4 and 7 in the evening. Journalists won't have enough time to submit a narrative for the following day's daily publication if it is afterward or earlier than that.
- The media officer who is familiar with the journalists will begin and guide the event in the ideal scenario, which

involves numerous participants. There ought to be 1 or 2 notable individuals there who would each make a 10-minute speech on the subject (initiative, release, contribution, inauguration or something comparable). The facilitator will then offer the media the chance to ask any remaining queries. Overall, it must be completed in 45 minutes. Personal interviews may then be conducted afterward.

- At conferences, a press kit is typically given out, which includes a press release, information about the conference's organisers, a report, study findings, statements, a list of specialists, and so on. Particularly videotaped or photographic content is occasionally shared. If a media source did not provide a representative for the event, one must provide the press kit to them by messengers after the event.
- A press conference must, in the words of journalists, 'yell for a headline', that is, there ought to be breaking news reported on them. Reporters will remember if a briefing is called but if there is no such information; there is a possibility that following, especially if there is breaking news, no one will attend the session. Press conferences are so common that media companies frequently dispatch inexperienced reporters to cover events.
- If at all feasible, press conferences must be replaced with press events. But there are a few technological considerations to make if one chooses to plan a press conference. These are as follows:

Checklist of the Media Conference

Location

- Easily reachable via public transit
- A parking spot is accessible
- The precise location, telephone and fax numbers are shared
- A registration office with a staff greeting and welcoming journalists at the entry

- Translating service if international journalists are anticipated

Site

- Will there be adequate outlets for TV crews?
- How robust are the fuses?
- How many guests are permitted?
- Camera station and photographers beside the journalists; Desks and seats in the appropriate numbers and positions
- Examine the heating and lighting
- Is there a photocopier on hand?
- Press kits on a table
- Members' desks with seating areas
- Where will the members approach from and exit from?
- Water cups containing water on the recipient's desk
- Is there a distinct space designated for private interviews?
- Where is the restroom?

Audio and Video

- A drop-down menu containing the members' names over the firm-action logo
- LCD, video and transparency projectors
- System on desktops, laptops and monitors: Windows or another?
- Participatory microphones as well as a movable microphone for inquiries from the floor
- Audio equipment
- Audio, video or photographic capturing?

During the Press Conference

- To keep track of attendees, maintain a sign-in form for the media and any other guests.
- Let journalists know how long the presenter will have at the start of the press conference, and be ready to end inquiries at that point.

- Limit the length of the media conference and announcements. An executive who delivers a brief announcement and answers queries will likely be more well-received by the media than one who delivers a statement for half an hour.
- Give space for queries.
- Capture the official's comments so that they could be recorded for record forever.
- Obtain answers to open-ended queries. If a query is posed to an authority that she or he is unable to respond to, she or he ought to acknowledge the difficulty and assure the journalist that the facts will be provided before the journalist's due later that day.

After the Press Conference

- To ensure that it is broadly accessible, post a translation of the media briefing as quickly as you can on your website.
- Provide any interested journalists with handout resources and a translation if they were unable to present yet were interested in the topic.
- Meet all deadlines for delivering promised information or answers to unresolved queries.
- Verify every stage of the process and then compile the observations for the upcoming conference.

Press Interview

Interviews are a tool used by journalists to obtain facts and develop their articles. It is the fundamental instrument for collecting news and a fantastic way for the business to reach out to its targeted audience with its content. A company can use media interviews to promote its positive image to the viewers. Because of this, here is certain advice for media interviews:

- Never take a chance. Planning is essential for delivering messages well. Engage with your internal public relations staff or a skilled media instructor to put effort and time into practice sessions. Ask your partner, your romantic partner or a reliable friend to grill you. Prepare yourself for difficult or aggressive queries by creating and perfecting concise, truthful and suitable responses.

- Start modestly. Before making it huge, test out smaller locations. Trade exhibitions are an excellent place to start if you want to hold a lot of media conferences using a group of reporters who are normally rather cordial. Keep your emotions under control. Even if it's natural to feel anxious, avoid displaying anxiety or uncertainty through body language.
- Take charge of the interview. Make an assertive introduction and then start the greeting. Ask a couple of straightforward queries to the interviewer right away, like who else they've talked to and how much duration they will require. By doing this, you take control of the situation and demonstrate your engagement in it.
- Refer to important facts as frequently as you can.
- Cut back on interruptions. Lend somebody else your smartphone and beeper, or switch it off.
- Look the reporter in the eye. Do not glance at the camera if the journalist is there. Maintaining eye contact is essential for conveying a strong and upbeat attitude. Gazing down could let you appear unresponsive while glancing at the outside environment can give the impression that you are being evasive or shifty.
- When answering a query, avoid repeating a negative remark made by the interviewer. Constantly use a positive tone when responding.
- Steer clear off of abbreviations, business lingo and jargon. The people are receiving the facts you provide through journalists. It is crucial to choose the language that everybody can comprehend.
- Do not ever guess. It is natural to do your best to think of a response, but being overconfident in a press interview could damage the image of your company. If you are not sure, admit it and commit to giving your best to learn the solution and return to them.

- Be accommodating, but never lose sight of your goal. You are not there to simply respond to the interviewer's queries; rather, you are there to make your main points known. Even though you shouldn't be sneaky, you should always be sending signs.

Seminar

A seminar comprises a discourse where the findings of an in-depth study or research are delivered orally or in documented papers. The primary goals of a seminar are to exchange information and hear the opinions of others with similar levels of expertise. Typically, the main research is presented by one speaker and then that work is thoroughly discussed. The audience members converse with the presenter and offer their opinions on what they heard.

- A seminar is typically a type of intellectual contact that is provided by an institution or by a business or professional group.
- It serves the purpose of convening smaller teams for regular sessions that each focus on a different topic and require active participation from all attendees.
- A relatively official presentation of the study or an extended conversation with the seminar presenter or faculty are two common ways to do this.
- To ensure that things are finished on schedule, create a timeframe for organising your seminar starting from the date of the event.
- Typically, attendees should have some background in the topic being discussed. The purpose of the seminar approach is to familiarise learners with the technique of their selected field in greater detail and to provide them the opportunity to communicate with instances of real-world issues that are constantly encountered during the study.
- Fundamentally, it serves as a forum for discussion, question-asking and debate about the required texts.

- In comparison to the lecture-based approach of professional instruction, it is comparatively informal.

Workshop

A global meeting or educational session that lasts for days is referred to as a workshop. In speaking, it is more work-focused, with all group members participating and being guided by specialised asset people. It stresses problem-solving, practical instruction and participant participation. When there is a real demo present, a symposium, presentation or conference frequently turns into a workshop.

1. Begin the workshop by wishing everyone a good time. Be kind yet influential in your conduct. Display compassion, adaptability, enthusiasm and a positive attitude.
2. Explain to members the session's subject and your intended workshop format.
3. Spend roughly 5 minutes outlining the main challenges related to the workshop subject.
4. Encourage other group members to share their opinions on the topics being discussed to learn from the team's encounters. Pose queries of people who could connect their expertise to the questions being addressed instead of controlling the discussion.
5. Keep talking about the main concerns and subtopics until everyone's attention is high.
6. Ask attendees for queries, and if they don't respond, start a dialogue by addressing specific members by their name (if possible).
7. Prevent one point of view from taking control of the conversation.
8. Guarantee that everyone has a fair amount of time to discuss the topics that are important to them.
9. Guarantee that the voluntary participation you designate makes details of the workshop's main themes. They can use this information to report at the session afterward.

10. Express gratitude to attendees for their involvement and focus at the global meeting's conclusion.

Conference

A conference is a private meeting. A conference is typically a sizable global meeting of people who come together to discuss a specific subject or to share knowledge or expertise. A conference might well be conducted to share opinions on a challenge the company is facing or another topic linked to it, and it could even offer a remedy, yet the conference's recommendations are not legally enforceable. They resemble suggestions more than anything else. The attendees of the conference must enrol to attend.

The salesperson might organise a weekly global meeting with the salespeople to review the previous week's revenue and formulate a plan for the upcoming one based on their opinions. A conference might occasionally be conducted to teach new hires. These workers may attend a conference where the company's essential facts are conveyed to them, and through conversation in a casual setting, they are encouraged to understand everything about the company, its goals, policies, and so on. This type of conference could be categorised as an educational conference.

In the event, that a significant business issue will take the lead and call a meeting to address issues of shared significance with representatives from other, smaller business issues. The host company chooses the conference location, arranges for the representatives' accommodations, creates a thorough schedule, invites notable figures to moderate different sessions, chooses the presenters, and after the conference transmits the documentation to major newspapers outlining a few of the conference's key points. These gatherings often last for 2 to 3 days.

In essence, global meetings rely on active communication, emphasizing direct, in-person connections within company tiers. These meetings involve oral and textual communication, covering announcements, agendas, minutes and reports. Meetings categorised by goals and types address education, comprehension, opinion gathering, knowledge sharing, change adoption, conflict resolution, decision making and optimism fostering. The meeting procedure includes notices, precise agendas and recorded minutes. Effective media management involves concise and newsworthy press releases, detailed press conferences and strategic interviews. Seminars present research findings, workshops are practical problem-solving sessions and conferences are large gatherings for knowledge exchange. The structure and procedures of a meeting depend on its type and purpose, showcasing the significance of effective communication in diverse organisational contexts.

Activity

1. Explain the significance of oral communication in global meetings.
2. Why is it important to have a direct, in-person connection in global meetings?
3. What are the different types of global meetings based on their goals?
4. According to W.H. Newman, what is the definition of a committee?
5. Why spontaneously occurring groups are not considered committees in the research context?
6. What advantages do meeting participants gain from receiving the agenda in advance?
7. Provide a definition of a press release and elaborate on its role in corporate communication.
8. Explain the distinction between a press report and a press release.
9. Examine the main goals of a seminar.
10. Cite examples of situations where a conference might be organised.
11. Outline the crucial elements involved in organizing an educational conference.
12. Describe the purpose and key features of a press kit distributed during a press conference.

17

Negotiation Skills in a Multicultural Context

With the risks so high, among the most crucial components for effective international business connections are negotiation skills. Even if you're the most skilled negotiator at residence, you must begin all over again when you enter a new culture and frequently have to practice ignoring everything you know. Your successful negotiation strategies, which are based on widely recognised trends and habits in your native nation, may not translate well in a multicultural context.

■ Negotiation Skills for China

If you are from another country, you may find the regulations governing business in China to be confusing and difficult to follow. However, when getting ready for your next negotiations, there is little you cannot acquire and comprehend.

Pay Attention to Individuals

You should start your negotiation procedure with the idea of building solid connections because China is a very relationship-based nation where individuals and their connections are valued more highly than the task at hand. This has an impact on a variety of communication-related issues when you are negotiating in China. Initially in the sense that individuals ought to come first in all that you try to accomplish. You build trust and a solid connection initially, and just after that, you shift to the cold reality.

There's another meaning to putting people first: you take note of collective dynamics. Determining the decision maker and the team members who typically have an interest in decisions and can affect their results is a smart concept.

Examine the Details Behind the Words

The Chinese prefer to present it elegantly. An enormous amount of thought passes into how you convey yourself to avoid any uncomfortable circumstances since the connection comes first. Gaining the ability to communicate in this manner is one item; comprehending their communication is quite another.

Pay attention and be aware that, should the situation warrant it, you will not receive a sure, callous no, but rather a tastefully attired and tactfully phrased no.

If you are accustomed to clear-cut, binary communication, set that aside and focus on nonverbal cues when honing your bargaining techniques in China.

Conversations about how excellent your business is and how much you've accomplished, the scope of an agenda you have, and overall projecting an air of ultra confidence are all necessary components of successful bargaining, but not in China. Here, humility does pay off. While this does not imply shying away, it does imply that you may appear more professional if you are prone to say less and maintain a low-profile during negotiations. Here, patience is appreciated just as much as modesty.

It won't be possible to cover everything in a few hours. Recognize that, since we are dealing with a relationship-focused nation, bargaining requires time, frequently a lot of it. There are numerous meetings, which allow people time to get to know each other and build confidence. Consider your moments as an investment, show that you are prepared to engage on an individual basis, and avoid coming across as hurried.

■ Negotiation Skills for the Netherlands

A crucial element of your business achievement is tailoring your negotiating strategies to the nation you are getting ready to grow into. While certain techniques require patience to master, others are simple to put into practice.

Straightforward Method

Negotiating with the Dutch requires a direct approach because they are renowned for being honest. If you were raised in a similar culture, this may come more naturally to you. If not, it may be more difficult if you are accustomed to extremely formal, indirect interaction in negotiations.

You will have to be direct in your communication of your desires when in the Netherlands. Express your thoughts clearly. They'll follow suit, and you'll be obligated to do the same.

Steer Clear Off of Superiority

The Dutch approach to living and working is based on an egalitarian viewpoint, so anything that could imply superiority must be avoided. You have not forgotten about rigid structures in Dutch businesses because everyone participates in the procedure for making choices, literally.

Don't talk to the manager, speak to the team as a whole, and be mindful of how your behaviour conveys that you value their opinion as much as yours.

Avoid Being Too Emotional

Don't let feelings come into it. If something is about operating in the Netherlands, then that is all there is to it. Especially when engaging in negotiations in the Netherlands. All that matters is that you and they both have goals that you and they both want to accomplish. This may come across as icy or even impolite to a few, but that is not the point at all. The task and outcomes are the goals in the Netherlands, and that is what matters.

Additionally, you must be willing to express your opinions honestly and you should not feel frightened when a variety of occasionally opposing viewpoints are expressed. Express your thoughts without holding back, even if they diverge from those of others. For negotiations to be effective in the Netherlands, everyone involved must share their opinions and thoughts openly and honestly.

■ Negotiation Skills for Germany

Organisation, self-control, timeliness, statistics and truth are of utmost importance. Being so straightforward, it frequently comes across as brusque. When discussing the German approach to employment and business, these are a few of the initial things that spring to mind.

Factual Data

Make sure to organise everything, paying careful consideration to data and facts. In Germany, building a personal connection or winning your spouse over with a polite conversation is not how you win someone over. The most valuable resource in any negotiation is the data you are prepared to provide, supported by hard data and statistics. Make sure your language is unambiguous and leaves no space for misinterpretation. Additionally, be prepared to respond to inquiries and to answer them. Anything ambiguous should be avoided.

Adopt a Formal Approach

In addition to being respectful of protocol, be prepared to adopt a completely formal demeanour when negotiating in Germany. You have to change your viewpoint if you're from a culture where individuals typically handle matters casually and on an individual basis, disregarding protocol. Due to the complex procedures of analysis and scrutiny, as well as the structural dynamics within a business, this degree of formality also affects the procedure for making decisions, which is frequently more gradual than in other European nations.

Prevent Being Ambiguous

Keeping things clear requires asking queries, when necessary, in addition to providing as much data as possible. If you think something is still wrong, don't be scared to ask questions. They'll follow suit, so it won't be viewed as rude. Since you both want to have clear phrases, queries are crucial to the negotiating procedure on both ends.

■ Negotiation Skills for Japan

To put it briefly, karaoke, regard and structure are key elements. Although extremely complicated, Japanese negotiation culture is also very simple to comprehend if you begin to pay focus.

Recognise Hierarchy

In Japan, respect and order are highly prized. Similar to the community at large, businesses are structured into rigid structures, with the importance of treating people with respect increasing with their rank or position in the hierarchy. Accordingly, you must familiarise yourself with the organisation's precise order, recognise the senior participants and conduct research on the business before engaging in any negotiations.

However, exhibit the same behaviour about your business: it is anticipated that senior executives attend the initial conferences to introduce themselves and the business as a whole to the prospective collaborators. Though their attendance at the initial meeting is crucial, they are not required to be available for all subsequent ones.

Win Over the Group

In Japanese businesses, team spirit is just as important as hierarchy as defining principles. You must be conscious of how drawn out and intricate the Japanese decision-making procedure is.

Since the Japanese value agreement, they will deliberate over decisions for as long as it takes to come to a decision. They will bring it up again and again, so it helps to be conscious of this. This means you can assume that they are still discussing the matter if you are waiting for a response, rather than necessarily knowing that it is a no.

This is the exact cause, too, that you shouldn't concentrate solely on one individual during negotiations. Instead of trying to persuade just one person, you must concentrate on the team as a whole. Since they won't agree on anything until everybody is on board—you want to persuade them all.

Accept Invites

Most of the time, the Japanese will extend an invitation to you for karaoke nights. For them, this is very significant since social interactions beyond the workplace foster the camaraderie and personal ties that are fundamental to their corporate and professional cultures. Heavy drinking is usually involved on these karaoke evenings, which doesn't look bad the next day. They use this as a means of decompressing and forging closer bonds with one another.

They will extend an invitation to you, and if you turn them down, it will be interpreted as a reflection of your lack of commitment to doing business with them.

■ Negotiation Skills for Saudi Arabia

Developing a network and comprehending whom to connect with are two of the most important skills for successful negotiation in Saudi Arabia.

Create Meaningful Connections

All business dealings and negotiations in Saudi Arabia are predicated on confidence. This has its roots in the profound connection values that characterise the nation's outlook on life, the workplace and business. Because Saudi Arabia is a relationship-based nation, confidence is established by first forging a personal connection.

Communicate to your collaborators that you are not just considering them as business associates and that you are keen on getting to know them as people.

Negotiation in Circles

If you're used to direct negotiations, the Saudi Arabian approach might seem unusual to you. It is typical for them to switch topics and then come back to where they were. Negotiation is not a linear process, so it is helpful to be aware of this type of communication so that you are not caught off guard.

You should be open to letting things happen as they come to you, and never forget that they prioritise over tasks and outcomes. Therefore, if the negotiations begin to take an unforeseen turn and things are bouncing around, don't show any signs of irritation or impatience.

Respect

Respect others and their customs and beliefs. Respecting individuals is essential in Saudi Arabia since interpersonal connections and networks are so significant. Discover their customs and standards of behaviour. You should also familiarise yourself with their forbidden subjects when it comes to addressing personal matters. Inform them that you are ready to follow their regulations and that you have arrived organised.

In conclusion, effectively navigating international business connections hinges on robust negotiation skills, a critical component given the inherent risks. Even if you're a skilled negotiator in your home country, entering a new cultural terrain often requires a fresh start, necessitating the ability to set aside familiar practices. Successful negotiation strategies rooted in your native country's norms may not seamlessly apply in a multicultural context. For example, negotiating in China prioritises relationship-building, while in the Netherlands, a direct approach is critical. Germany emphasises formality and reliance on factual data, Japan values hierarchy and group harmony, and Saudi Arabia focuses on creating meaningful connections and respecting local customs. Adapting negotiation techniques to specific cultural nuances is imperative for successful international business endeavours.

Activity

1. Why are possessing negotiation skills essential for establishing effective international business connections?
2. What are the fundamental elements of negotiation skills emphasised in China?
3. How does the Netherlands culture shape the negotiation approach?
4. In what way does China prioritise relationships in negotiation processes?

5. Why is it imperative to steer clear of emotional involvement in Dutch negotiations?
6. In Germany, how does the level of formality impact the dynamics of negotiations?
7. How does the straightforward expression of opinions impact the negotiation dynamics in the Netherlands?
8. Why is it crucial to respect customs and beliefs in business interactions in Saudi Arabia?
9. How does the prolonged decision-making process in Japan affect negotiation outcomes?
10. Why is it crucial to familiarise yourself with the precise organizational structure in Japan?
11. Why is it important to show regard for customs and beliefs during business engagements in Saudi Arabia?

Part VII
Technology in International Business Communication

18

Digital Communication Tools and Platforms

Introduction

In this day of communication, having accessibility to a lot of information is regarded as prosperity. The use of information-retrieving methods, which have made significant contributions to the development of modern communication technologies, is among the foundations of this type of resource.

Given extensive international business activities, the application of novel communication technologies can address a few of the fundamental issues, including precision, expense, velocity, quality and volume. Therefore, in today's complicated commercial organisations, where communication must reach a broad geographical area both in and out of the nation, the need for alternate means has become essential. In numerous international businesses, communication methods other than the usual ones including television, radio, computers, sound/visual tapes, video discs, telecommunications and numerous mechanical components have been utilised effectively. They are beneficial for administrative tasks like organisation, management, guidance and incentive, among others.

It would be challenging to remain in the competitive environment if international business does not utilise new technology for communication to assist the population as a societal obligation.

Everything that takes the shape of the Internet and might have numerous lines connecting one another is referred to as a network. A network in the context of a computer setting refers to a link between several machines both inside and external to the company. An electronic network consists of interconnected nodes or pathways that are capable of communicating with one another. Possible international business norms are the linkage of numerous electronics or peripheral equipment at dispersed places that send data required to carry out network operations. The network of electronic communication is the linking of all different channels. A well-connected computer network, therefore considers multiple pathways. It stands for a unified operating system. A contemporary complicated organisation may include several dispersing sites linked by other sites, which suggests the possibility of a network.

Networking Characteristics

1. It aids in establishing and sustaining external communication using a third-party organisation.
2. Recasts management as a function and completely changes the manager's job.
3. Professionals in any area can communicate with one another.
4. Increasing staff productivity allows for the eventual goal of fostering networking within the company to be accomplished.
5. The availability, real-time nature and ongoing improvement of the informational calibre of international business data.
6. It expands the number of devices or endpoints connected and enables communication between the set of particular networks.
7. The network system enables data to be distributed in a timely, rapid and effective manner, especially in the situation of multinational organisations with a worldwide workforce that operates in numerous different nations.

Networking Benefits

1. It is quick and simple to exchange data between multiple electronics.
2. Fast and simple accessibility to data and its instant availability aids in boosting output.

3. It reduces the amount of work required to complete documentation.
4. F2F engagement is made possible by technologies; it spares workers a significant amount of effort and time.
5. It is simple to notify all of the dispersed personnel about any modifications to organisational policies or procedures.

Intranet

The term *intranet* refers to a link to the web within the company. It is also known as a platform having a limited population. Selected personnel inside the organisation receive well-managed and organised data via the intranet platform. The Internet can be accessed via the intranet, yet not the other way around. Entry to the intranet is constrained or exclusive. Intra alludes to personal networking *within* a company.

An intranet is an inner webpage utilised by a company to provide business-based data and information to workers. Numerous international businesses have been looking for new strategies to enhance staff communication in recent times. To distribute content more effectively and thereby cut down on overhead expenses, the deployment and use of the intranet is indeed a viable alternative.

Intranet Benefits

1. Reduces the expense of business communication by up to 60 percent.
2. Raises workers' levels of effectiveness and production.
3. It gives individuals a means of quickly getting the knowledge they require whenever they require it.
4. Regardless of the hardware technologies they use, every employee of an organisation has the chance to use the intranet's technologies and to view the data held by the business.
5. The intranet transforms the traditional paper workplace into an electronic workplace by producing electronic files for possible international business communication.
6. Intranets reduce obstacles to open communication within organisations, enabling both people and groups to interact and exchange information.

Internet

The abbreviation 'net' is used to refer to the global network now known as the Internet. The Internet is made up of several tiny networks and other smaller, globally dispersed linked computers. The World Wide Web and cyberspace are accessible through it. So, it is an international network of interconnected, autonomous computer groupings. Two-way communication is possible on the Internet. A customer's computer screen becomes a window to the entire globe as they explore the Internet's possibilities. The transmitter and the recipient must be located on a similar system line for the Net to function.

To describe it plainly, the Internet can be compared to the telephone network, which also serves as a means of international communication. Connecting to the Internet can be done in numerous different methods. Likewise, various kinds of programs can be run. A channel or means for numerous systems to connect is the Internet. A product's integrity and ability to compete and offer value on the global marketplace determine its performance in the industry. The existence of a given product featuring precise characteristics, cost, usability and other attributes must be made known to the possible worldwide user in a worldwide marketing arrangement.

Benefits of the Internet

1. Messages can be sent and received worldwide over the Internet.
2. Having data saved on the systems for later use.
3. Perusing periodicals like magazines and newspapers.
4. Obtaining content that we find interesting, including publications.
5. Using e-banking, which is the practice of managing one's bank account through online means.
6. Shopping online allows consumers to conserve time.
7. Upgrading business with the most recent technologies available worldwide.

E-mail

Using a system of telecommunication and computer connections, customers can receive and send information using electronic mail or e-mail (a network of electronic communication). The message could be composed of brief remarks and congratulations, lengthy text documents with visuals and photographs, video recordings or sound or just plain content. E-mail is an 'electronic post office' because of this. Even without a receiver on the other side, it enables communication. It entails that one can deliver e-mails whenever the user wishes and at any moment. The recipient of the text may read it anytime she or he chooses. As a result, for that specific communication, the transmitter and the recipient do not need to interact at the same moment.

SMS

The ability to transmit and receive textual messages from and to portable devices is known as SMS. Short textual message exchange between mobile handsets is made possible via the SMS communication system. 2.4 billion active customers or 74 percent of all smartphone users, utilise SMS textual messages as their primary method of information communication, making it the most popular data app in the world. The content could be expressed as a string of letters, figures or both. Regardless if a data or voice call is currently in place, a portable device that is in use can send or receive a brief message using SMS at any time.

Advantages

- A message may be transmitted at any moment,
- It is useful in an emergency and
- It saves both money and effort.

Disadvantages

- Extremely brief words or lines can occasionally be misunderstood by the recipient.
- Network congestion causes a lag in the text's transmission.

Teleconference

Teleconferencing is the digital exchange of messages involving two or more individuals in different places. It can be described in its most basic form as the long-available teleconference call. The number of users can indeed be significantly expanded if speakerphones are installed in every workplace. All parties can communicate with each other when employing two-way communication. Oral messages such as announcements from a corporate president are conveyed concurrently to numerous places during one-way communication conversations.

Merits

1. Simple to utilise.
2. It is simple to get.
3. Simple to take part over any mobile connection in the globe.
4. Setting up a meeting room takes only a short amount of time.
5. Time, money and resources are saved.

Demerits

The fact that F2F communication between individuals cannot be replaced by teleconferencing is a significant drawback. Teleconferencing won't be effective when individuals would rather connect in person.

Figure 18.1: Teleconferencing

Source: https://knowledgeplace4all.blogspot.com/2019/01/what-is-teleconferencing.html

Videoconferencing

Videoconferencing is an ongoing video chat involving two or more people or involving two or more places. Individuals in distant places can view and hear one another simultaneously through videoconferencing. It is entirely interactive and resembles F2F discussions in many ways. Based on the number of technologies employed, it might be an interacting connection between two places or it might be a broadcasting video, where the site doing the broadcasting sends its picture to several other places that might be capable of communicating back via a regular telephone connection. It is feasible to link the 2 sites so that everyone can view and understand one another, simulating an actual meeting, using more sophisticated systems and devices.

Advantages

1. It replaces direct communication between people.
2. It offers real-time communication.
3. It solves distance-related obstacles.
4. It results in reduced executive travelling expenses.
5. It results in time savings for conferences.
6. It enables individuals seated in various locations to quickly expand their expertise.

Disadvantages

1. The individual the one wishes to speak to must possess the electronic and conferencing-specific gear and software.
2. A computer cannot be carried about like a mobile phone. Consequently, it has an impact on how portable the conferencing is.
3. A videoconference's confidentiality is not often ensured.

Best Practices for Effective Digital Communication

By integrating the following best practices into your digital communication strategy, you can elevate the effectiveness of your messages, promote positive relationships, and contribute to a more collaborative and streamlined communication culture.

- Design your intranet as a centralised hub for information sharing within the organisation. Ensure that important documents, announcements and resources are easily accessible to all employees. Give preference to creating a user-friendly interface for the intranet. A positive user experience, boosted by intuitive navigation, personalised dashboards and well-organised content, enhances overall adoption rates.
- Keep your online content updated regularly. Follow Internet and web accessibility standards, provide alternative text for images, and ensure that your website is usable by everyone, regardless of their abilities.
- Crafting a clear and succinct subject line is a crucial best practice in e-mail communication. As the initial element recipients encounter, the subject line plays a pivotal role in determining whether the e-mail is opened. It is essential to create subject lines that precisely convey the e-mail's content and purpose, enabling recipients to grasp its significance. To promote transparency and assist recipients in prioritizing and organising their e-mails effectively, it is important to steer clear of ambiguous or deceptive subject lines. By following this guideline, you increase the chances of your e-mails being read and comprehended promptly.
- SMS messages are usually brief due to character limitations, making it essential to communicate information succinctly. Concentrate on crucial details, avoiding unnecessary elaboration. If a message surpasses the character limit, assess whether it can be condensed without losing meaning. Clarity and conciseness in SMS messages improve readability, guarantee timely communication of vital information, and increase the likelihood of effectively engaging recipients.
- An essential recommendation for effective video-conferencing is to have an ideal lighting setup and background. Sufficient lighting is crucial for participants to see you clearly, promoting better engagement and understanding. Position yourself in front of a natural

light source or utilise well-distributed artificial lighting to prevent shadows on your face. Furthermore, select a neat and uncluttered background to reduce distractions and uphold a professional image. A well-lit and carefully arranged video setup not only improves your visibility but also plays a key role in fostering a positive and focused virtual meeting experience for all participants.

To sum up, in the digital age, information access is considered a form of prosperity, driven by technologies like the Internet and communication networks. In the realm of international business, adopting novel communication technologies is essential for addressing issues like precision, cost, speed and quality. Various methods, such as intranet, e-mail, SMS, teleconferencing and videoconferencing, offer distinct advantages and drawbacks, facilitating global connectivity and real-time interaction. Best practices for digital communication, including user-friendly interfaces, regular content updates and effective subject lines, contribute to organisational efficiency and collaboration. Embracing these technologies is crucial for businesses to stay competitive and fulfil societal obligations.

Activity

1. What role does an intranet play within a company?
2. How does e-mail serve as an electronic post office?
3. How does videoconferencing facilitate individuals situated in diverse locations to replicate a real meeting experience?
4. Why is the arrangement of lighting and background essential for ensuring successful videoconferencing?
5. Why is the adoption of modern technology essential for successful international business communication?
6. What are the pros and cons linked with the utilization of SMS messages in communication?
7. What are the recommended best practices that can be integrated into a digital communication strategy to improve its effectiveness?
8. How does the Internet facilitate worldwide access to messages and information?

19

Managing Virtual Teams and Remote Communication

Introduction

It should come as no surprise that most businesses today are looking for fresh, creative approaches to increase their efficiency and competitiveness and that these frequently entail utilizing emerging technologies. Without a doubt, the way most businesses operate has changed significantly because of the introduction of novel information and communication innovations. Businesses are changing how people interact with one another, which is changing how individuals perform their jobs. The work environment of today is entirely distinct from what it was even a few decades ago.

The utilization of virtual teams is one of the modifications that have been implemented in the last few decades. Conference calls, teleconferencing and telecommuting have been used by businesses for a long time to help employees perform their jobs in an easier way, and effectively and economically. But virtual teams go above these developments as well.

It is now feasible for groups to collaborate on projects even when they are not colocated in the same place. Individuals can indeed collaborate on initiatives from various locations—even across the globe if needed—at various moments and even from times that vary. Groupware and other software breakthroughs, along with Computer-Mediated Communication (CMC) innovation, enable people to collaborate on projects, track employment and investments, communicate both within and across the team and manage a together-created core record or project.

Maintaining cooperation and effective communication within a team is never easy, but in virtual teams, these problems are much more significant. It is widely acknowledged that maintaining regular communication among individuals within a business is crucial, but despite advancements in communication technologies, this is becoming more challenging in most businesses nowadays.

It is common for team composition to fluctuate based on requirements, even in normal colocated teams. Nowadays, it's also typical for teams to include experts or participants who work as team members but are not affiliated with the parent company. Their inclusion in the team stems from their possession of knowledge, abilities or experience that the team needs and that they might not have within the company. Additionally, it is typical for employees to collaborate on multiple tasks and participate in multiple teams at once. Work teams have traditionally worked on distinct initiatives with beginnings, ends and finite life spans. Big, dynamic initiatives that adapt and change to fit the needs of the moment are becoming more and more prevalent. Considering the various forms of complexity and difficulties that now plague numerous, if not most, groups, one can see how rapidly the degrees of difficulties rise significantly when one adds the additional issues of having groups that are dispersed (not colocated), functioning at various hours, possibly functioning from various nations and time areas, and even having various spoken languages. One fascinating feature of modern businesses is the prevalence of several reporting ties and supervisors for various initiatives that employees work on within teams or matrix-style businesses.

Virtual Teams

Virtual teams are being used far more frequently these days, and not just in the high-technology sector. They are now employed by a wide range of businesses. The physical constraints of time, place and business barriers are not an issue for virtual teams. They streamline timetables for projects, cut down on facilities and travel expenses, and enhance communication and decision-making processes by utilizing electronic collaborative tools and other strategies.

Virtual teams consist of team members, a type of computer-mediated communication facilitating interactive engagement, and a software system enabling them to collaborate on a project concurrently from different locations and at various hours. This setup allows effective and valuable monitoring and incorporation of operations. .

Nowadays business settings are more favourable to remote work and virtual teams due to a variety of modifications and variables. These possibilities become even more appealing as businesses become more globally scattered and interact with individuals in various places and time areas. These teams are not only desirable but might even be required when companies combine, buy out other companies, get acquired by another company or outsource work to various locations across the globe. The choice to employ these novel team management techniques will also be influenced by other considerations such as reducing expenses. Undoubtedly, a lot of businesses are discovering that working virtually and from home can drastically cut down costs and time while also enabling more strategically concentrated travel. Employing these teams can frequently shorten the period to market, which can greatly benefit clients.

Virtual teams come in a wide variety. They may be, and frequently are regular work teams, but they may also be executive teams or even teams consisting of executives from various locations within the same company. In the virtual community, a brand-new team structure known as the 'community of practice team' is also beginning to take shape. This is a situation where a collection of individuals from various businesses come together to encourage each other's work, even if it is being done for various businesses, and may be functioning on associated initiatives or issues.

Management of Virtual Team and Remote Communication

It is easy to focus on technological advances when thinking about virtual team management. While this is vital, it is also essential to remember that social systems are the primary component of virtual teams, just like any other team. The performance of a team will thus continue to rely on the calibre of data that is accessible, how it is shared and employed, and how the team members employ the data to accomplish their operations, despite the communication's technological advances or software and hardware that the entire team employs to accomplish their tasks. No group can compare to the calibre of its participants and data. In a team, one anticipates that the performance will showcase the synergy that develops from the group into a functional societal employment package. Nevertheless, this does not happen on its own; rather, it requires cooperation, communication, building trust, sharing knowledge, training and exceeding individual performance.

In all honesty, based on our observations, not numerous businesses nowadays do team-based management models extremely well. First off, even though a lot of businesses discuss encouraging teams, they hardly ever give them the power they require to carry out their duties. This is a widespread issue in a lot of businesses. This is a bigger issue with virtual teams because in the conventional position of manager or supervisor, the manager is expected to give the team significant autonomy over their work. If this isn't the case, and the manager is required to be active in every aspect of the decision-making process, they become the bottleneck that keeps the group from operating at its best. To accomplish its objectives, a virtual team is required to be equipped with sufficient assets and the power to employ them as needed. Furthermore, our observation is that the majority of businesses continue to structure and operate around individual positions rather than groups. Supervisors still frequently view teams as an array of tasks instead of as a collection of interrelated, cooperative coworkers collaborating on a shared objective.

Empowerment is another element that can be crucial in virtual teams. If applied correctly, this could be very advantageous for remote teams. Supervisors of virtual teams might function better if they organise team operations as opposed to leading them. A democratic authority direction, a low degree of engagement, self-regulation, boundary-spanning and willingness to assist team members in any way required are traits of an empowering and encouraging manager.

Although they may differ slightly from those found in traditional face-to-face teams, a lot of the tasks required of managers in virtual teams are nonetheless equally crucial, as previously stated. Managers need to make sure that everyone feels like they belong on the team. To further improve their understanding and expertise, they must also participate in the team's activities as both a respondent and a spectator. Empowerment and this kind of involvement go hand in hand, and when managers don't perform up to par, it's usually because they aren't included in the group dynamics. To encourage and promote improved group operation, managers must be involved in the dynamics and know about what is happening. Additionally, by participating in the dynamics and acquiring knowledge and experience, the manager builds trust with the team members, who are then more inclined to pay attention to her or him and ask for guidance or assistance.

There are a lot of tasks that managers need to do to set up the environment and offer the assistance that healthy, productive virtual teams need to handle them efficiently. Kimball (1997) offers the following actions that managers can take to support the success of the virtual team:

- *Goals*: since there aren't enough face-to-face conferences, teams should plan more often and have clear check-ins to ensure that everyone is working toward the same goals.
- *Roles*: managers need to ensure that every member of a team has an established position that is comprehended and embraced by all; this role can be selected or emerging, but it needs to be explicit. This is because role uncertainty and disorientation are typically linked to poor efficiency.
- *Culture*: Every team must operate within the framework established by the business's dominant culture.
- Technology should be employed to help the virtual team integrate into the culture, but it's also important to acknowledge and address the ever-evolving connection that exists between the team and the culture—that is, how the team both influences and is influenced by it.

- Managers need to facilitate and promote dialogue, debate, inquiry and other forms of group interaction. Technology should not just be utilised for data interchange and archiving.
- *Feedback*: Invest time in employing technological advances to enhance team member communication; this is the main means to generate regular, insightful and prompt comments. The elderly members, who might have less time with CMC, are probably the ones who will find this most significant.
- Managers have to make an effort to ensure that work is completed at an appropriate rate. Some users will likely use the shared space more frequently than others. You do not, nevertheless, want certain participants to feel as though they are falling behind. Keeping individuals engaged, on board, and they feel a sense of belonging, like they belong to the team in an asynchronous setting, is difficult but crucial.
- The concept of access and re-entry applies to virtual teams as well. Imagine joining a swift-moving river and having to swim to catch up with the people who were before you. Managers must endeavour to update and integrate prospective or returning participants into the procedure promptly and efficiently.
- A networking term for the procedure of compiling and combining various replies in virtual teams is called *weaving*. This implies that you have to inform individuals of their current location, where they were in the past and potential future destinations.
- *Participation*: Managers must understand the distinct signals that distinguish between people who are involved and contributing to a virtual team and those who are not. Nonverbal signals are more prevalent in face-to-face groups, making it easier to gauge the degree of involvement there. However, supervisors in virtual teams still need to be capable of spotting these signals.

- Emoticons are textual representations of mood or feelings, and other 'para messages' that can enhance a lean communication style, but their usefulness depends on the comprehension of the intended audience.
- *Movement*: The team's manager needs to know what is going on (or not) in the group. Virtual teams will experience periods of high activity and low activity, just like any other team. Although this is typical, the supervisor still needs to keep an eye on things and oversee the workflow to ensure that the team is collaborating effectively.

To summarise, businesses are increasingly adopting emerging technologies that are reshaping work environments. Virtual teams, facilitated by technology like groupware and CMC, enhance efficiency and address modern workplace challenges. These teams operate across locations, offering benefits such as streamlined timelines, cost reduction and improved decision making. Successful virtual team management requires a balance of technology and social dynamics. Empowering teams, setting clear goals and roles, fostering a conducive culture, and leveraging technology for communication and feedback are essential. Managers must actively participate, promote trust and monitor team dynamics. Strategies such as goal setting, role definition, cultural integration, facilitating dialogue, providing feedback, managing work pace, ensuring accessibility and monitoring team movement contribute to success. Overall, effective virtual team management demands a holistic approach integrating technology and social dynamics for a collaborative and high-performing virtual work environment.

Activity

1. Why is the involvement of managers crucial in virtual team dynamics?
2. What elements make up virtual teams?
3. How does empowerment play a crucial role in enhancing the effectiveness of remote teams?
4. Which factors contribute to the increased advantages of remote work and virtual teams?

5. What benefits do 'para messages' offer in the communication of virtual teams?
6. Share five tips for enhancing remote team communication.

20

Social Media in Global Business Engagement

Introduction

Social media, as an indication of digital transformation, is one of the present-day megatrends influencing international business. Social media is linked to globalisation processes and international business as a result of execution, speed, site and entry-point decisions, foreign market education and expertise recombination. Social media has become important in terms of the reach of assets and skills in the home and host sectors, and it impacts companies' ability to handle the risks of foreign players and outsiders.

Businesses and academia have shown a keen interest in social media. The advent of social media has drastically altered the way individuals and businesses connect and engage. Social media platforms like Instagram, Twitter, Facebook, YouTube and LinkedIn offer virtual spaces for social interaction and career development.

They contain a vast amount of user-generated data, which may aid businesses and researchers in better understanding human conduct. For various businesses, social media offers a means to establish, share and handle interactions and operations with their individuals, clients, suppliers and other stakeholders. These novel forms of media have generated a plethora of novel possibilities as well as novel business structures that threaten conventional business practices.

Views of Social Media in Global Business Engagement

Social media is regarded as an intriguing and effective tool for establishing globalisation methods, effectively exploring foreign market possibilities, and utilizing scaling to expand in multiple geographic marketplaces. Similarly, research indicates that social media can be used to accelerate globalisation and enhance business performance in foreign marketplaces. Current research demonstrates the significance of social media in global business through concepts like these. They do, however, raise queries about how these things occur and whether the connection is as unquestionably advantageous as the literature suggests.

Social Media and Business Global Operations

The papers on social media in global business highlight certain elements that appear to be specially declared for this arrangement. The initial problem is that the study usually presumes that social media affects global growth instead of vice versa. Secondly, it appears that there is an urge to emphasise the beneficial features of social media and global endeavours instead of the (potentially) negative aspects. While all the works investigated raise at least a few beneficial difficulties.

Marketing: Most of the research on social media in global business is concerned with global marketing. Because social media is simple to implement and does not necessitate expenditures in marketing assets, it is not unexpected that this research views social media as an expanded marketing asset through which businesses may connect with prospective consumers and produce broad international contact at an affordable price. Social media has evolved into an element of globally incorporated marketing communications, shortening, or eliminating geographical distances and enabling communication with clients by spreading knowledge and enabling the sharing of goods and information.

According to some investigations, market consciousness can generate buzz, enforce virtuous loops and boost speed because posts may become popular instantaneously. Also, businesses can use social media to safeguard and communicate their brand. Businesses can use social media to construct and reinforce their global brand image. International businesses can also use social media to gain access to systems. It enables businesses to establish and oversee an extensive variety of connections quickly, strengthen current connections, preserve customer engagement, and build mutual dependents with clients and business partners. According to the literature, intimacy, paying attention, communication and individual tones in discussions are examples of social media components that help businesses create customer engagement and loyalty. Direct communication with clients all over the globe provides the chance to form long-lasting, emotional bonds. Prior research additionally indicates that social media may be employed efficiently to gather market data for marketing purposes.

Aside from marketing, social media is closely linked to several aspects of sales. According to investigations, social media is a truly modern sales channel. It allows you to contact salespeople in foreign markets, encourages client segmentation and sales focus, and may be employed at various phases of the sales procedure.

Sales: Likewise, to marketing, the utilization of social media decreases the requirement for human sales resources because businesses may reach prospective customers or suppliers via social media platforms. As a result, social media offers inexpensive sales assistance, assists in generating additional inquiries and lowers transportation expenses. A strong attachment to the brand fostered by social media utilization encourages more often buys and greater quantities, resulting in higher interest and sales, which improves the business's overall efficiency. However, higher demand may result in a lack of resources, and the difficulties of employing social media become visible in noticed sales. Due to the unpredictability of social media, requirements may rise to the point where the business is unable to respond. Failure to satisfy demand may result in a drop in sales afterward if customers begin to avoid the company. Furthermore, a company's online contacts must be often efficient or they may lead to adverse outcomes. In the context of globalisation, the requirement for direct revenue staff and intimate connections grows in tandem with foreign growth. Also, factors such as ambiguous security and confidentiality, poor transportation, or an absence of a web encounter could decrease revenue.

R&D: Previous research on social media and global business emphasises heavily on global sales and advertising, but less on the relationship between social media and R&D in a global setting. Given the extensive research on the close connection between advertising and R&D, this is quite unexpected.

Considering global business, current literature recognises that social media may supply businesses' R&D functions with global market data and consumer suggestions that may be utilised to create novel, tailored and improved goods. Social media creates novel possibilities and novel business models. With this view, R&D is transforming, at least in part, from a product-centred framework to an experience-centred model. Businesses can translate market insights into goods and services that clients are prepared to pay for. Because social media allows for direct communication with clients, businesses employ it as an instrument for incorporating clients into the development of goods. In the global setting, social media may encourage customer-focused collaboration and innovation. Businesses may allow clients to develop their distinctive goods, or they may produce and distribute goods on request, resulting in reduced expenses in terms of storage.

However, social media may pose a trap for innovative businesses because it can direct R&D and manufacturing in areas where the business lacks sufficient skills. Too much emphasis on customer desires is hazardous, but it is possible if social media becomes too prominent as an origin of concepts. Given that user conduct is beyond business management, social media may result in circumstances where businesses' R&D operations are jeopardised. Innovative customers, for instance, may tamper with exclusive goods and generate a product that the business does not want.

Human resource management: Their problems are addressed in social media studies of businesses' global operations. According to the literature, social media is associated with job searching; businesses can utilise it to attract exceptionally qualified and focused human resources (HR). Social media gives businesses easy accessibility to talent databases, which may help with talent acquisition. When employing social media for recruiting purposes, expenses are typically kept low.

Social media is useful in hiring circumstances, but it may also have broader uses. Social media can help expatriates with their well-being, transfer of expertise, adaptation and job performance in multinational corporations. Social media systems can be a source of solid employment-related support, assisting the assignee to achieve greater degrees of achievement even when the job is performed remotely. Online social media platforms, as a key characteristic, foster social elements of teamwork, cooperation and collaboration, which may reduce dissatisfaction and increase comprehension.

Nevertheless, cultural disparities may continue to impede positive interaction, and care must be taken in how social media is employed. If the business's assets and skills are insufficient, this will be a challenge. For instance, it appears that digital natives are far more acquainted with social media than upper management. Higher-ups may, paradoxically, regard social media as a frivolous hobby of adolescents and, as a result, forbid their staff from employing social media platforms at employment. The top management's view of social media is critical, and it must be viewed as an instrument of strategy.

In essence, social media plays a pivotal role in the digital transformation impacting global business, closely tied to processes of globalisation. Platforms such as Instagram, Twitter, Facebook, YouTube and LinkedIn are reshaping communication, providing virtual spaces for interaction and professional growth. Businesses leverage social media to gain insights into human behaviour through extensive user-generated data. It is a critical component in global marketing, sales, R&D and HR. While presenting opportunities for globalisation, market exploration and expansion, social media also poses challenges, including demand management, security considerations and addressing cultural disparities. Effective strategic management is crucial for harnessing the full potential of social media in engaging with global business.

Activity
1. In what ways does social media affect international business with regard to execution, speed and entry-point decisions?

2. How has the emergence of social media altered the manner in which individuals and businesses establish connections and engage with each other?
3. How does the influence of social media affect a company's ability to handle risks related to foreign entities and external individuals in both domestic and overseas sectors?
4. What considerations should businesses be aware of in employing social media for recruitment purposes, especially in terms of costs and talent acquisition?
5. How can businesses leverage social media insights for innovative product development?
6. Why is the perspective of senior management on social media essential in human resources management?

Part VIII

Building and Maintaining International Business Relationships

21

Trust and Relationship Building Across Cultures

Relationship Concepts

The concept of social exchange, which contends that every measure within societal categories may be clarified by communications between people, serves as a basis for different research studies on connections. The transfer of both material and intangible operations between multiple individuals is referred to as social exchange. Social interaction strengthens relational conduct, but it may additionally end in an absence of societal strengthening. Relationships may end because of infrequent social contact.

Later concepts, like the societal entry concept, clarify how societal connections grow. According to the societal entry concept, trust can lead to the growth of loose connections into closer interactions. Social reinforcement plays a significant part here, along with self-disclosure acts, which are measures that indicate responsive personal data to other people. Receiving beneficial encouragement from another person leads to increased self-disclosure to the other individual. These measures improve when both people have a positive attitude toward the connection. As a result, the more intimate the connection, the more prepared both parties are to reveal personal data.

The uncertainty reduction concept is a critical concept for understanding the significance of interaction and data delivery. This theory addresses the difficulty of anticipating another person's conduct and activities. When a person is extremely unsure about the counterpart's future conduct, she or he is more likely to seek additional data. In contrast, if the level of ambiguity is inadequate, little additional data is needed.

Uncertainty may be minimised via effective communication and nonverbal cues. Enhanced communication reduces ambiguity and the necessity for seeking additional data. As a result, communication is essential in developing long-term connections between two people. Two kinds of connections exist between businesses. Initially, there is a connection between people from a single business and people from another business, and then there is the organisational connection between two businesses. As a result, when extending across cultures, it is critical to determine which of the two kinds of connections a company has to deal with.

Relationship Across Cultures

Businesses are typically connected to business systems. Long-term connections can help companies gain access to outside assets by allowing them to join these networks. External assets may be critical for businesses that thrive in a foreign setting when extending internationally. As a result, businesses must gain entry to these regional business systems.

Also, networks in a foreign nation can mitigate risks associated with unidentified marketplaces. Businesses with a strong link to the regional marketplace may be able to expand their business possibilities. This is because locals possess an excellent grasp of market preferences and also a cultural comprehension.

Vendor and buyer connections have grown increasingly important, particularly in emerging nations, and they gain advantages from interlinked systems of regional businesses. Building relationships in these sectors necessitates frequent communication. Businesses are frequently unable to create a suitable relationship with locals throughout the globalisation of a business. The main barrier to globalisation is the absence of understanding of cultural disparities and prevalent business procedures.

While working in a foreign marketplace, businesses usually acquire via expertise. Experience can help businesses better assess business possibilities by establishing important connections with locals who may subsequently offer essential data about market trends. Higher encounters can thus lead to less ambiguity when conducting activities in a foreign nation. Ambiguity in relationship building may be detrimental to both the foreign partner and the business. Hazard related to connection ambiguity is among the primary variables influencing the achievement of a business's globalisation. The Grammarly-sponsored *The State of Business Communication 2023* report shows that 1 in 5 business leaders claim to have experienced a loss of credibility due to poor communication.

As a result, businesses must mitigate the danger as much as feasible. A foundation of trust between foreign collaboration and the business wishing to grow globally is one helpful risk-mitigation approach.

The Concept of Trust

According to Wikipedia, trust is "a psychological state comprising the desire to embrace danger depending upon beneficial standards of the intent or conduct of another". Thus, trust relates to the perception or feeling that a person can put their trust in a different individual or business, knowing that he or she will not be disappointed. It is critical to examine the two primary elements of the description stated previously. The first is concerned with the capacity to place yourself in a powerless state in a dangerous situation. The second component is a sense of optimism about the result of this situation.

It takes a lot of trust to think that another person will do everything in her or his power to make sure nothing malicious is done. This trust will be determined by who is accountable for a person's health. The said object may be another human being or a business. As a result, trust may be classified into two categories: social trust and organisational trust.

There are some challenges to building and maintaining trust between businesses. Two individuals engaged in business are frequently frightened of the other side abusing the trust that is involved in data and sharing of assets, among other things.

These individual communications are the instruments that assist in developing societal trust as an initial foundation for two businesses to begin building a closer relationship. When supervisors from two distinct groups raise their mutual communication, expertise and comprehension, they will start to understand how much they can trust the other person and determine the conditions under which this trust may be considered secure. As a result, a social trust may be defined as a 'conditio sine qua non' condition for achieving organisational trust.

Trust in Cross-Cultural Relationships

The range of this research includes the formation of relationships while performing business overseas. The capacity to build and sustain trust through cultural barriers is critical to the achievement of this process. As a result, a natural propensity among people is to form more powerful relationships with others with whom they share a prevalent culture, as mutual ideas are more plausible. As a result, it is appropriate to suppose that fellow citizens are a lot more inclined to establish trust among themselves than in cross-cultural relationships.

Furthermore, various cultural settings have developed via an informal sequence in which inherent characteristics trigger a specific category to act in a particular manner. These differences are the driving force behind the gradual growth of trust between people from various cultural backgrounds. As a result, cultural differences in establishing trust play a significant part. It has been demonstrated that cultures produce trust in various threats. For example, particular cultures trust each other even before they know one another because they share a membership category. Other cultures, on the other hand, trust an unidentified someone depending on the likelihood of sharing interpersonal characteristics.

When attempting to bridge the cultural divide, depersonalised trust can be extremely useful. Depersonalised trust is the degree to which people choose to trust a person they do not know personally yet. When executed with people of identical national origins, this situation becomes even more difficult when employed in a cross-cultural setting. Such distinction is based on the fact that cultural ties facilitate the formation of trust between fellow citizens. However, if done properly, this trust may contribute to the development and maintenance of exchanges between foreign businesses, thereby strengthening the relationship.

Nonetheless, it has been demonstrated that the country of origin (COO) may serve a significant part in the growth of cross-cultural trust and may decrease the hazards related to unfamiliarity. When growing overseas, businesses should assess their COO's image and the business's general perception of the foreign marketplace. This can provide the first indication of a potential early existence of trust in the nation that is hosting. This occurrence is related to prospective customers' perceptions of risk. As a result, in a sector where hazard is a major factor, the COO can provide insight into the likelihood of initial trust that exists in the marketplace.

Furthermore, it has been discovered that COOs may assist businesses with brand perception and brand. Some geographical areas have an already existing reputation in the lens of society, thereby offering a business with extra credibility based solely on its source, instead of its performance. The cultural gap between both sides concerned has been recognised as a component that impacts the level of trust instead of an element that reduces the relationship between trust and performance. It is critical to remember that in each international relationship, one side is recognised as being stronger than the other.

As a result, businesses must focus on attempting to discover an ongoing equilibrium and establishing mutual trust to cross the cultural divide. As a result, mutual trust between respondents is crucial for successfully conquering possible disagreements between cultures.

Understanding Cultural Distinctions

Aside from the previously discussed variables of relationships and trust, the final factor that is important in this investigation is culture. The idea of culture is stated as the group coding of the awareness that differentiates the individuals of one category or class of individuals from other people. As a result, culture cannot be confused with character or personality, as these characteristics are unique to each person. The idea of culture may be linked to multiple kinds of categories like ethnic groups (e.g., groups), nations (in governance, administration or social science) and businesses (which relate to both social science and administration).

Trust-building Exercises and Activities

Establishing trust-building activities is crucial for effective international business communication, contributing to the cultivation of positive relationships, increased collaboration and the prevention of potential misunderstandings. One impactful strategy involves conducting a cultural exchange workshop where team members from diverse cultural backgrounds share insights into their customs, communication styles and cultures. This initiative promotes cross-cultural understanding, thereby minimizing the risk of misinterpretation and building trust through increased awareness and empathy.

Introduce a worldwide buddy system, pairing team members with counterparts from different locations. These pairs collaborate on specific projects or tasks, fostering a one-on-one connection. This initiative encourages transparent communication, as buddies exchange insights into their work culture, daily routines and professional challenges. The personal connections developed through the buddy system contribute significantly to creating a more supportive and trusting environment across the entire international team.

Employing simulated business scenarios is an effective way to build trust. For instance, the creation of a cross-cultural negotiation simulation allows team members to practice and enhance their communication skills within a controlled environment. This activity serves to highlight potential challenges in international business transactions and provides participants with a platform to learn from their experiences, ultimately nurturing trust through shared learning.

Team building retreats create a relaxed and informal setting for team members to connect outside the formal workplace setting. Involvement in team-building activities, such as tackling challenges or participating in recreational events, assists in overcoming communication barriers and facilitates the development of personal connections. These connections frequently translate into increased trust and improved communication as team members resume their work responsibilities.

Technology's Role in Building Cross-cultural Trust

Technology serves as a potent facilitator in fostering and cultivating cross-cultural trust. It achieves this by offering tools and platforms that streamline communication, enrich cultural comprehension, and encourage collaboration within diverse cultural environments.

Technology aids in advancing diversity and inclusion efforts by providing specialised software that assists organisations in overseeing and evaluating their advancements. These tools play a role in establishing inclusive environments and fostering trust among diverse teams.

Technology enables the implementation of cultural sensitivity training initiatives via e-learning modules. These programs assist individuals in acquiring a deeper understanding of diverse cultures, norms and communication styles, thereby nurturing cultural awareness and encouraging trustworthy interactions.

In cross-cultural business dealings, Blockchain technology improves transparency and confidence. It furnishes a secure and verifiable transaction record, diminishing the likelihood of misinterpretations and conflicts, especially in the realm of international business.

Technology acts as a driver for intercultural communication by supplying tools, such as instant messaging and video conferencing, enabling real-time communication. This facilitates consistent and direct interactions, assisting individuals in surmounting language barriers and cultivating a feeling of connection and trust.

In summary, the concept of social exchange, explaining measures within societal categories, forms the basis for relationship studies. It involves the transfer of material and intangible operations between individuals, impacting relational conduct. Concepts like societal entry, uncertainty reduction and trust elucidate how connections evolve. Trust is crucial in overcoming disagreements and building mutual trust in cross-cultural relationships. Cultural differences, COO and technology play significant roles in fostering cross-cultural trust. Technology such as Blockchain and e-learning, streamlines communication, enriches cultural comprehension, and encourages collaboration within diverse cultural environments.

Activity

1. What is the definition of social exchange within the context of relationships?
2. How does trust contribute to the transition from casual connections to more intimate interactions?
3. How does the uncertainty reduction concept enhance our comprehension of the significance of interaction and information sharing in relationships?
4. Why is it crucial for businesses to identify the nature of their connections when expanding across cultural boundaries?
5. What is the significance of cultural exchange workshops in building trust in international business communication?
6. Why is it essential to differentiate between culture and individual traits like character or personality when examining relationships, trust and business dynamics?
7. How do simulated business scenarios help build trust in international teams?
8. How does technology contribute to fostering cross-cultural trust by streamlining communication and encouraging collaboration?

22

Networking and Relationship Management in Different Countries

Networking and Relationships

In recent times, networking has grown more essential in the business setting and management. With the rise of distinct social media of various orientations, networking has shifted significantly. Nevertheless, the word networking essentially implies managing every kind of professional relationship, not just on social networking sites, but additionally personally. Soft skills such as networking and relationship management are required of an effective project supervisor since they are frequently critical to project performance. Relationships should be developed, preserved, and nurtured to assist themselves, one's professional life and one's initiatives.

Building a network between individuals entails having the possibility to utilise synergies and exchange concepts with experts from multiple areas. The desire to network stems from the desire to gain several benefits through multiple contacts. Contacts may assist in addressing issues, answering queries, offering concepts, and ultimately, completing a project since they offer essential data or support differently. If you have a large network of contacts, you won't have to spend time looking for data. Personal relationships make things simpler, as encounter indicates that queries from friends are dealt with far more quickly than queries from outsiders. Numerous investigations have been conducted to investigate the significance of relationships and a lot of them have found that relationships can account for as much as 60% of a business's achievement. Relationships benefit everybody, regardless of their profession. Last but not least, in the majority of instances, those with solid connections and a person to speak for them are provided with positions and advancements. As per an investigation conducted by the Hans Böckler Foundation's Economic and Social Science Institute, approximately one-third of all positions are posted and packed in some manner through relationships.

Networking abilities are also valued by workers. People like functioning with sociable individuals, so if you are friendly and outgoing, you tend to be a far superior project manager. One can begin at various levels by encouraging one's networking ability. According to one concept, you are linked to every person on the planet via an average of six knots. So everybody knows a person who understands a person who recognises a person who knows a person, and so on.

By 1974, early scattered studies on business marketplaces in the United States and Europe had proven that buying was a multiperson action, clients were frequently hesitant to switch vendors, and there was an unexpected level of reliability and long-term viability in their relationships with a lot of their vendors. Even big, strong clients often sought collaboration with vendors instead of ruthlessly and independently utilizing their purchasing authority in the marketplace. Collaboration established via relationships frequently included system modifications and goods and services modifications by both vendors and consumers.

Different theories for these occurrences were put forth in Europe during the 1970s, based on studies carried out in Sweden, the United Kingdom and France. It was clear that growing market focus, leading to several strong competitors, gave a more limited choice of partners, and the significant increase of variation of stakeholders became increasingly important. Risk perception and methods for reducing risks were two potential causes. In investigations of business purchasing conduct, significant expenses of transition (changing expenses) and significant resource commitment and inertia were identified. It was also clear that shoppers take a proactive approach to locating vendors and shaping their relationships.

By 1975, these investigations had resulted in the realization that supplier-customer relationships were complicated issues and that separate investigations of purchasing conduct or marketing operations ought to pave the manner to investigations that concentrated directly on the trends of communication between the two stakeholders in a relationship.

'The relationship between businesses, regardless of their proximity or distance, serves as a repository for the respondent's collective encounter. The relationship is made up of discovered regulations and standards of behaviour. It creates the environment in which people's instances take position. Negotiations, settlements, shipping and social relationships are examples of these instances. Every instance impacts and is influenced by the whole relationship. Also, relationships develop and may be thought to progress through a set of phases marked by increased mutual modification, decreased distance and increased dedication.

The relationship is not a binary factor, and the query for investigators is not if a relationship is present in any particular scenario. In a similar vein, it is not an inquiry if businesses ought to create a relationship in an individual situation for businessmen. Relationships exist in a broad spectrum of shapes, and the goal for investigators is to comprehend the essence of the relationships. Inter-company relationships are intricate.

Relationship Management Procedure

Krapfel et al. (1991) refined the strategic method of buyer/seller relationship management. They propose an approach in which kinds of relationships and relationship management methods are organised collectively to determine the best relationship portfolio. Transaction expenses are considered in this survey. They additionally understand the significance of corresponding relationships and signalling intent to collaborators as an element of the relationship management procedure. They consider signalling to be a vital element of the procedure for adaptation. Two variables influence the relationship kinds they detect (partner, friend, connection and competitor): relationship regard and curiosity similarity (similarity of a business's financial objectives with its view of its prospective partner's financial objectives).

The relationship management methods proposed are cooperation, bargaining, handling, rule, accommodation and submission (again, discovered 2-D by perceived authority place and interest similarity).

Turnbull and Zolkiewski (1995) use an experimental evaluation of a big UK computer vendor to evaluate portfolio designs. While they discovered the Shapiro et al. classification of clients to be most suitable for the investigated business, they believe that a 3-D grid with the expense to provide, net price and connection value would be more useful as an advertising evaluation and planning instrument in general.

Despite these rather standard customer-based management outcomes, this study shows that asset allocation choices are frequently made without an exhaustive examination of the possible hazards to every relationship. This is due to at least two factors. First, whether at the person or group threshold, relationship evaluation is a necessary prelude to expenditure and managerial decisions. Individual evaluation is probable to be both feasible and useful for businesses with a handful of significant relationships. Individual evaluation is not probable to be possible in businesses with lots of connections. As a result, it is critical, albeit uncommon, for businesses to establish a structure for the classification of connection kinds to aid in evaluation. Secondly, relationship portfolio management invariably includes decision making. This is possibly the hardest component for managers to deal with. Relationships between UK grocery producers and significant retail store categories provide a fascinating illustration of this problem. These manufacturers are very keen on developing their relationship with specific retailers and have, in numerous instances, expanded the relationship as the section for evaluation from sales operations into marketing decision making. Nevertheless, developing a closer relationship with one hold category, which might include product alterations, exclusiveness, joint marketing, and so on, inevitably calls for an extent of commitment that will require the business to embrace a more detached relationship with other people.

Certain executives find it hard to comprehend the scope of this dedication and the expenses related to it in other relationships. Their unwillingness could be motivated by a realistic assessment of the possible advantages of additional dedication.

Nevertheless, if the vendor is unable to pay the expenses of having a stronger connection with a single client (partly stated in terms of a more distant relationship with others), then the vendor has to embrace the constraints of that relationship in terms of client dedication for inventory stages, data, and so on. If it fails to gain approval, the executives engaged are bound to have two prevalent self-delusions. The initial point is that their relationships appear to be 'nearer' than they are. The second prevalent misconception is that relationship management is simply being pleasant to clients. This viewpoint is incorrect for a minimum of two distinct causes. Initially, niceness requires assets, and businesses are not likely to have enough assets to be nice to all. Secondly, if utilised by all customers, the degree of gentility shown to each individual is not likely to be important.

Network Management

We previously stated that it is not possible to analyse any inter-company relationship in loneliness, both analytically and managerially. Other businesses impact relationships by interacting with and influencing the participants in dyadic communication. Early IMP studies concentrated primarily on dyadic relationships, and the majority of the concepts and experimental study cases provided were about relationships with only two groups. This was due to the approach employed and the explicit choice to initially concentrate on the dyad while acknowledging that relationships are frequently, if not constantly more complexly linked. Turnbull and Ellwood (1984) pioneered the method by studying the interactions of international revenues affiliates and agents.

Likewise, both conceptual and experimental studies grew out of the realization that individual relationships were unable to be fully comprehended apart from the other relationships in which every participant participated, as well as the impact of relationships that enclosed them in the larger network of relationships. This has resulted in the creation of a network system and dynamics concept. However, experimental investigations have not always kept up with the rate of theoretical growth in the network domain. As a result, the network research frequently fails to offer a clear description of network events, let alone rules for managerial decision making. The network viewpoint, on the other hand, provides an effective structure for analyzing business scenarios. It emphasises the variety of impacts on individual businesses and relationships, and also the nature and effects of various activities taken by relationship respondents. However, it adds another layer of complication to the explanation of business market conduct and the comprehension of buyer-seller relationships.

In conclusion, networking, crucial in contemporary business, has evolved beyond online platforms, extending to personal interactions. Essential for effective project management, soft skills contribute significantly to project performance. Studies highlight that relationships account for a substantial portion of a business's success, emphasizing their importance. Valued by employees, sociable individuals are deemed better project managers. The interconnectedness theory suggests that everyone is connected through an average of six connections. Early studies in the 1970s delved into buyer-seller relationships, emphasizing collaboration and system modifications. The relationship management process involves categorizing relationships, considering transaction costs, signalling intent and employing various methods. Network management acknowledges the interconnected nature of relationships, offering a framework for analyzing business scenarios, though practical decision-making complexities persist.

Activity

1. Which essential interpersonal skills are critical for effective project supervisors and why?
2. What theories emerged in Europe during the 1970s to explain changing dynamics in business relationships?
3. What does the concept of being connected to every individual on the planet through six degrees signify?

4. Why do Turnbull and Zolkiewski (1995) prefer a 3-D grid, considering the expense to provide, net price, and connection value, over Shapiro et al.'s client classification for marketing evaluation and planning?
5. What makes personal relationships crucial in streamlining tasks and acquiring information more efficiently?

23

Case Studies of Successful International Business Relationships

International business relationships are now a standard instead of an occurrence in a growing globalised globe. Businesses continually search for ways to broaden their reach and enter novel markets around the globe. While entering the international market can be difficult, there are many instances of businesses that accomplished extraordinary results. These accomplishment instances can be used to teach striving international businessmen.

McDonald's

McDonald's is frequently based on the collection of successful international business relationships. McDonald's has evolved from a small business in the US to a worldwide fast-food restaurant chain with outlets in more than 100 nations.

McDonald's international success is largely due to the following variables:

Regional Taste Modification: McDonald's possesses an aptitude for modifying its menu to regional preferences. In India, for example, where a lot of individuals are vegan, they have a variety of alternatives for vegetarians such as the McAloo Tikki burger.

Local Partnerships: McDonald's frequently has stakeholders like regional businesses and business owners who comprehend the culture and marketplace dynamics, assisting in the navigation of regulation obstacles and the establishment of an effective regional presence.

Quality Consistency: While adapting to regional preferences, McDonald's holds strict quality requirements around the world, guaranteeing clients have a consistent encounter.

Coca-Cola

Coca-Cola, the legendary beverage business, is another effective example of international growth. Coca-Cola goods can be purchased in almost every nation on the planet and the brand is well-known worldwide.

The following are critical success variables for Coca-Cola's international business ventures:

Coca-Cola's solid brand identity and compatible communication have enabled it to connect with clients all over the globe. The iconic red logo and memorable marketing have crossed cultural and language boundaries.

Regional Advertising: Coca-Cola tailors its advertising strategies to regional cultures and preferences while preserving an international brand image. In commercials, for instance, they frequently characterise regional famous people.

Coca-Cola's wide distribution network guarantees its goods are accessible in even the most distant edges of the globe.

Samsung

Samsung, a South Korean group, is an excellent instance of a business that has accomplished international success in a variety of sectors, ranging from gadgets to shipbuilding.

The following variables contribute to Samsung's worldwide success:

Samsung is well-known for its constant inventiveness and capacity to remain ahead of the market developments. This invention has enabled it to gain market share in a variety of product groups.

Studies and Development Capital: Samsung invests strongly in R&D, permitting it to create innovative technologies and goods that are appealing to worldwide customers.

International Manufacturing Presence: The business has production plants and affiliates in several nations, enabling it to manufacture goods for regional markets while upholding high-quality standards.

Control in E-Commerce: Alibaba

Alibaba, established in China by Jack Ma, is an extraordinary instance of an e-commerce behemoth that has broadened its reach far beyond its homeland.

The following are important variables in Alibaba's international success:

Alibaba's websites, like Alibaba.com and AliExpress, link consumers and vendors from all over the globe. This international business has aided its international growth.

Payment Methods: Ant Economic (now referred to as Ant Group), Alibaba's economic subsidiary, created Alipay, a platform for electronic payments that assisted international deals and made it simpler for international clients to make purchases on Alibaba's systems.

Strategic Investing: Alibaba made strategic investments in a variety of international electronic commerce and technological advances firms, broadening its scope and impact beyond China.

Toyota

Toyota, a Japanese automaker, is well-known for its international automotive management and cutting-edge manufacturing techniques.

The following are critical success variables for Toyota's international business ventures:

Toyota has an image for creating high-quality, dependable automobiles that are appealing to customers all over the globe.

Effective Manufacturing: Toyota's production structure, also known as the Toyota Production structure (TPS), lean production and effectiveness reduce expenses and waste while preserving quality.

Toyota has a significant foothold in significant marketplaces, with production facilities and sales networks ideally situated all over the globe.

These case studies show that successful international business relationships necessitate an array of variables, such as adaptation to regional marketplaces, a powerful worldwide reputation, inventiveness and strategic partnerships. Also, these successful businesses frequently share an unwavering dedication to standards and client contentment. International entrepreneurs can be inspired by these instances as they take on their worldwide business journeys, knowing that international success is attainable with the right methods and commitment to high standards.

Part IX

Managing Conflicts and Ethical Dilemmas in International Business

24

Identifying and Resolving Cross-Cultural Conflicts

Identifying the Cross-Cultural Conflicts for Better Business

With international business at a record-breaking level, conflict between cultural divisions will unavoidably weave themselves into operations and relationships. Before entering the arena of global trade, international business opens the gate to a completely novel set of cultural impacts that should be addressed with the greatest degree of investigation and assessment. Cultural conflicts can take many different shapes and types, ranging from big, intense debates to tiny, minute differences. To fully comprehend how an array of cultural conflicts may impact international businesses and their intended success, the international business professional should be capable of correctly differentiating the difficulties between approval or denial of distinct tastes and preferences, equilibrium for ethical standards and legal obligations, and tolerance or resistance of distinct principles.

In the end, most cultural conflicts stem from a capacity to separate the facts from the circumstances and find the truth as it truly is. As a result, deciding how to manage an efficient transnational business successfully and properly while accepting distinctions of views from place to place remains an issue. Recognizing the diligent occupation at hand may save numerous international business experts a great deal of labour in grabbing up the fragments after shedding to unanticipated hazards.

Initially, the kind of conflict that occurs as a result of accepting or rejecting various tastes and choices may be impacted by the degree to which both sides involved are willing to agree. Individuals from various cultural origins will have varying tastes and preferences, a few more straightforward than others. Opinions and tastes may be highly personal and specific, which allows supervision and prevention of problems. Individuals can choose to differ in these instances, even if they believe the opposing side is from a different planet. Nevertheless, these choices and tastes soon start to have an impact on others in extremely direct methods, making them more difficult to overlook and dismiss. At this stage, experienced international business executives must think quickly on their feet to find methods to resolve a dispute under greater stress and move beyond a potential stalemate scenario.

Second, the kind of conflict that naturally rises to the top of a reservoir of stress is the attempt to strike equilibrium between ethical standards and legal constraints. When choosing between moral and legal patterns, individuals must decide whether to adhere to their conscience or the laws and regulations that are already in place. The first tugs at the emotional strands of the heart, while the second tugs at the reasonable effects of implementation and penalty. The need to decide between ethical and legal behaviour often creates a dilemma that contradicts itself when the two structures include numerous inconsistencies, a situation that seldom arises in practical scenarios. To make things more severe, international businesses have to investigate what is ethical and legal in the nations included since norms vary widely and have a significant impact on the conduct of both sides performing business. An astute expert international business executive must learn to have equilibrium where their decisions will fail, either strictly adhering to legal guidelines or displaying an ethical code that transcends the law. Nevertheless, they will frequently prioritise the ethical instead of the legal, and subsequently their conscience over the strict law. Lastly, perhaps the most common in international business nowadays, the conflict over acceptance or intolerance of various principles represented by other cultures presents difficulties in establishing how much tolerance both sides will allot to the circumstance.

Numerous times, conflicts in international business are exaggerated when they might have been viewed as noncompeting principles. Cultures that take pride in their diversity and the incorporation of various points of view seem to generate the most conflict in this manner. They view the extent to which their team may be described as truly dynamic as exclusively advantageous, even though this exact component of their community shows out to be the source of the problems discovered. The irony is only mildly surprising. Furthermore, not every culture puts an identical amount of weight on particular principles, rendering the harmony of cultures offered by industrialization more challenging to attempt. In other words, both parties of the argument may hold the same significance, but the impact of the significance in decision making could be vastly different. Finally, an experienced international business executive must possess the qualities of morality and honesty, altruism, group drive and support, though the level at which each of these qualities is valued in every nation differs. In the international business environment, alter is the most secure path to conflict resolution, and the business experts in control of every scenario must be conscious of how their choices will affect the cultures engaged in every fight for limits.

Cultural Conflicts Measures

Various nations have distinct workplace norms. Enhancing current understanding of how to effectively handle business with an organisation from a foreign country can only advantage a potential business associate. So, how must a US-based international business plan deals with Germany, the EU's biggest trading partner? Initially and foremost, it's important to understand that "sequence, framework, accuracy and completeness permeate professional existence here, which is why foreigners in business settings could be excused for supposing their German colleagues possess a secret collection of regulations—and are subsequently them to the point".

The initial approach to making an adverse impact on a German business associate is to show up late for an appointment or to fail to make an effort to mitigate reputation impairment by contacting ahead with an acceptable reason. From here, continuing to use titles and surnames demonstrates honour for the German and a propensity to take duties and structure carefully. Lastly, a crucial tip for maintaining business with a German business is to express yourself with optimism and dependability, particularly through a firm handshake before and following an appointment, beginning with the most senior individual present and continuing down the hierarchy before departing. Finally, doing business with a German necessitates diligence, reverence for their customs and intent to maintain business apart from individual life.

Performing business with a Mexican business requires an entirely distinct set of considerations. Mexico is the USA's second-largest supplier of goods, trailing only China. Brazil is the biggest economy in Latin America, and it has been scaling the rankings for a long time. In opposition to common opinion, the Mexican economy is expanding considerably and is expected to maintain an upward growth trend over the coming decade. The first thing to remember when dealing with Mexican collaborators stems from their extremely personal culture: take the opportunity to build strong, long-lasting connections to demonstrate trustworthiness. Secondly, hierarchy is important in Mexican business, with most major decisions being taken by a small category of people at the highest level of the chain. This data cautions the foreign business partner to make certain they are working with the correct individuals to achieve the greatest outcomes in the shortest amount of time. Lastly, time-conscientiousness is not a critical piece of the business puzzle in Mexico, and agendas are frequently tossed out as discussions progress with adaptability (Business Culture in Mexico). Finally, the most successful Mexico-related business emerges when connections and structure take precedence over external needs, such as deadlines and personal obligations.

Finally, in the past few years, the Chinese marketplace has skyrocketed, rendering it an ideal location for strong financial growth and strategic business attempts. China has undergone speedy shifts in the market and an extensive array of legislative changes, prompting executives across the globe to want to take benefit of the country's constantly inexpensive manufacturing expenses. The first thing to remember when doing business with a Chinese connection is how significant personal relationships are to them particularly when dealing with decent individuals who show respect to those who deserve it. Since every connection in China is inequitable, it is critical to show sufficient respect and regard to those of age and rank, particularly if their view directly impacts any business being undertaken. Secondly, Chinese supervisors will be instructed and briefed, illustrating Confucian ideas that impact the community's power structure (Business Culture in China). Lastly, Chinese culture teaches that debts must constantly be compensated, so an individual who does numerous favours will be paid numerous favours. These types of relationships are always useful when aiming for the greatest feasible achievement in business affairs. In the Chinese culture, avoiding controversy while maintaining an excellent reputation will always get a business expert far; these are rules that any international business expert ought to bear in mind when doing business with Chinese businesses.

Conflict is a natural part of human character that will inevitably manifest itself in any sociocultural communication, corporate or casual. Individuals who say to have not encountered employment conflict are thought to be either existing in a dream globe, blind to their setting or confined to single isolation. Also, emphasizing cross-cultural conflict in business environments necessitates a deliberate and conceptual perspective on culture, cultural ideas and their associated descriptions, and cultural impacts on interpersonal relationships, conflict and its administration. Though most conflict has varying degrees of benefit to businesses, smart international business employees ought to comprehend how to manage conflicts that emerge to prevent any distraction from business objectives and purposes. As a result, the fundamental initial phase for any international company witnessing any level of cultural conflict is to perform a cross-cultural evaluation, which would research the parallels and contrasts of the individuals engaged in business relationships, from vendors to customers. Values, customs, signs of culture and language can all be considered in this investigation before the individuals engaged attempt to connect. Businesses cannot simply assume that their assumptions about specific cultural teams are always accurate without conducting thorough studies to see their principles and opinions in action. Businesses should operate to acquire a comprehension of both sides engaged and their specific positions anticipated and desired, only then businesses can properly comprehend a conflict. As an outcome, businesses performing international business have become conscious of the potential cultural barriers that may impede advancement and have planned accordingly.

In essence, in the current era of unprecedented global business, understanding and managing cultural conflicts is imperative for success. International business professionals must carefully navigate various conflicts, such as accepting or rejecting preferences, balancing ethical standards and legal obligations, and addressing the tolerance or intolerance of different principles. These conflicts often stem from the challenge of distinguishing facts from circumstances, making the efficient management of transnational businesses a complex task. Specific measures for managing conflicts in various countries emphasise the importance of adapting to workplace norms, building lasting connections, respecting hierarchy and considering time consciousness in different cultural contexts. Overall, recognizing and addressing cultural conflicts through thorough cross-cultural assessments is essential for international businesses to overcome barriers and ensure progress.

Activity

1. How can cultural conflicts become apparent within international business associations?
2. How do inconsistencies between ethical standards and legal constraints contribute to cultural conflicts in international business?
3. What strategies should a US-based international business employ when engaging with Germany, the largest trading partner in the EU, taking cultural nuances into account?

4. How can businesses proactively manage cultural conflicts in new global markets?
5. In business with China, how can one leverage personal relationships, adhere to Confucian principles, and navigate cultural expectation of reciprocating favours?
6. How can clashes arising from the acceptance or rejection of diverse principles by distinct cultures influence the overall success of business ventures in the realm of international business?

25

Navigating Ethical Challenges in Diverse Business Environment

The Dimensions of Ethics

Every culture has its own set of behavioural standards and guidelines depending on its ethical values. The ethical responsibilities and justice discovered within a community of individuals are correlated to the personal ethical framework every person holds and comes when facing the decision-making procedures of existence, which typically results in obedience to society. Though one culture is unlikely to have the identical collection of ethical guidelines and prevalent conduct as another, certain universal principles of ethics, like those coping with fraudulent behaviour, stealing, and so on, apply to all countries. These illicit behaviours are regarded as unethical in nearly every circumstance and are frequently classified as succumbing to fraud. Also, the business world places a high value on ethics because so much revenue is based on ethical principles and procedures, causing expertise and comprehending of these codes of conduct critical for the wellness of any international business. The advantages of doing business internationally are connected to the duty of learning foreign ethics since businesses that claim to be truly international need to have a comprehension of the ethical and legal loops in which their businesses operate. Any sign of corruption, combined with a sense of an absence of business societal duty may forever damage connections between international businesses and their customers.

For instance, the 3rd World governance may have no issue exploiting kids by causing them to work, but US experts might encounter serious allegations if they did business with firms that tolerated such an absence of ethical behaviour. In cases where there is extensive media protection, the American people can decide to boycott goods produced through such actions like abuse of kids, which conflict with the US administration's duties. Victoria's Secret, America's biggest lingerie seller is currently dealing with multiple assaults alleging that the business has passed away due to the previously disclosed trend of abuse. A great deal of the business's cotton originates from Burkina Faso, a country where child labour is becoming increasingly prevalent in the manufacturing of its main harvest shipping, cotton, since the labels 'organic' and 'fair-trade' cotton have become prevalent in the marketplace, urging an enormous level of abuse. Trade controversies such as the Victoria's Secret controversy can lead to businesses erecting trade obstacles and decreasing consumer demand. As a result, engaging with businesses with flaws in ethical practices may be harmful to international companies and even developing countries providing essential supplies for trade. Among the most recently stated causes of administrations not offering foreign help or urgently required debt alleviation is the prevalence of corruption since providing help to a foreign country led by corrupt officials would only exacerbate the moral decay already in place. As an outcome, ethics serve a significant part in the accomplishments of international businesses, prompting any international business supervisor to understand the importance of researching the ethical norms of the cultures with which they do business and to react appropriately when worries are elevated.

Businesses nowadays encounter a growing number of ethical challenges and duties. Businesses should navigate a variety of challenges to preserve their image and guarantee long-term viability as parties demand more openness, societal duty and ethical decision making. The difficulties that businesses face vary ranging from managing ethical obligations with economic objectives to determining the effect of ethical choices. We'll look at a few of the primary difficulties that businesses encounter when it pertains to ethics and business duty, as well as a few methods for overcoming these obstacles.

The Business Ethics Challenges and Business Duties

While business ethics and business duty are critical parts of any profitable business, they encounter several difficulties when it involves navigating these fields. Among the major difficulties are:

1. *An absence of transparency on ethical norms and instructions*: An absence of clear ethical norms and rules is one of the most significant obstacles that businesses face. While numerous businesses have an ethical or moral code, these may be vague or hard to enforce circumstances. This may render it hard for workers to understand the way to behave in ethical quandaries, resulting in insufficient decision making throughout the business.
2. *Stress to emphasise revenues over ethical concerns*: Another prevalent obstacle that businesses face is the urge to emphasise revenues over ethical reasons. In numerous instances, businesses must make hard trade-offs involving brief economic advantages and future ethical concerns. This may result in choices that emphasise profitability over other parties like staff, consumers or the surroundings.
3. *Trouble in determining the effect of ethical choices*: Evaluating the effect of ethical choices can additionally be a substantial challenge for businesses. While it is simple to determine the economic effect of a choice, it is much more difficult to evaluate the effects on other key players, like staff or the surroundings. This may render it hard for businesses to determine if they are engaging in ethical choices.
4. *Managing ethical obligations with other business objectives*: Lastly, businesses must strike a balance between ethical duties and other business objectives. A business, for instance, might be required to make hard decisions, such as if to spend in sustainability programs or prioritizing worker advantages. This can necessitate a delicate managing behaviour, making it hard to understand the way to value ethical concerns.

Overall, businesses face important challenges in terms of ethics and business duty. Businesses, on the other hand, may guarantee they are making ethical choices that match their principles and encourage their sustainable growth by comprehending these challenges and establishing methods for navigating them. In the following part, we will look at a few of the techniques that businesses may employ to deal with these challenges.

Methods for Navigating Business Ethics Challenges and Business Duties

While there are undoubtedly challenges for businesses in terms of ethics and business duty, there are additionally numerous methods that businesses may employ to navigate these difficulties. A few of the most efficient methods are:

1. *Creating a clear code of ethics and behaviour*: Creating a clear code of ethics and behaviour is among the most significant business techniques. This may instruct staff on how to behave in ethical challenges and guarantee uniform decision making throughout the business. This code must be particular and feasible, instead of ambiguous or general.
2. *Organising openness and open interaction with participants*: A further significant approach is to emphasise openness and open interaction with affected parties. This can assist in establishing confidence with consumers, staff members, and other key players, as well as guarantee that the business is held responsible for its activities. Businesses must be honest and open about their activities, even when the news isn't good.

Figure 25.1: Methods for Navigating Business Ethics Challenges and Business Duties

Source: https://management.org/blogs/business-ethics/2010/10/23/10-benefits-of-managing-ethics-in-the-workplace

3. *Ensure ethical decision making has been incorporated into business culture*: Businesses must also concentrate on integrating ethical decision making into their business culture. This includes incorporating ethics and business duty into staff training and growth, as well as guaranteeing that every staff comprehends the significance of behaving ethically. It also entails keeping staff responsible for their activities and fostering an environment of confidence and responsibility.
4. *Putting the desires of stakeholders ahead of brief economic advantage*: Ultimately, businesses ought to prioritise stakeholder desires ahead of brief economic advancement. This includes taking into account the effect of business choices on every key player, such as consumers, staff members, the environment and the larger group. Businesses may establish a foundation of confidence with clients and staff and guarantee long-term sustainable development by adopting a strategic approach and organising partner desires.

Overall, businesses can effectively navigate the difficulties of business ethics and business duty by implementing these methods. Businesses may establish trust with clients and staff by emphasizing openness, stakeholder involvement and a clear code of ethics, and ensuring they are creating ethical choices that match with their principles.

To summarise, each culture adheres to its distinct ethical values, shaping acceptable behaviours. Individual ethical frameworks contribute to adherence to societal norms, and while cultural guidelines may vary, certain ethical principles like those condemning fraudulent conduct have global applicability. In the realm of international business, where financial success hinges on ethical practices, involvement in unethical behaviours can severely harm relationships with clients. Businesses encounter obstacles, such as a lack of transparency, the pressure to prioritise profits at the expense of ethics, challenges in assessing the consequences of ethical decisions, and the need to balance ethical responsibilities with other business goals. Strategies for surmounting these challenges encompass the establishment of clear ethical codes, prioritizing the interests of stakeholders, ensuring transparency, and embedding ethical decision making into the corporate culture. Through the adoption of these approaches, businesses can foster trust with stakeholders and guarantee sustained long-term growth.

Activity

1. How do cultural differences shape ethical standards in global business communication?
2. Why is ethics crucial in international business, where revenue often relies on ethical principles?
3. How might trade disputes lead to trade barriers and decreased consumer demand, impacting businesses and the countries supplying essential trade goods?
4. How does the absence of clarity regarding ethical standards present a notable hurdle for businesses when making ethical choices?
5. How does strategic alignment with stakeholder interests build trust for sustainable development?
6. How does adept management assist businesses in balancing ethical responsibilities with other goals?

26

Case Studies on Ethical Decision Making

While navigating ethical difficulties may be hard, still many businesses have done it effectively. These businesses have built trust with consumers and staff by arranging openness, responsibility and partner involvement, and have established an excellent standing for ethical conduct. Here are some instances of businesses that have effectively navigated ethical issues:

1. *Patagonia*: Patagonia is a widely recognised outdoor clothing business that is committed to ecological sustainability. Several initiatives have been taken by the business to minimise its ecological effect, such as the utilization of recycled resources in its goods, the reduction of garbage and the encouragement of ecological reasons. Furthermore, Patagonia has been open about its ecological effect and attempts to mitigate it and has supported clients to fix instead of substituting their clothing. Patagonia has established an excellent standing for ethical conduct by emphasizing sustainable development and openness.
2. *Ben and Jerry's*: Ben & Jerry's is a well-known ice cream business that has a long history of supporting societal justice and ecological sustainability. To aid these aspects, the business has taken multiple actions, such as acquiring fair trade supplies, employing ecologically friendly wrapping and backing societal justice programs. Furthermore, Ben & Jerry's is open about its attempts and has been involved with clients and staff to guarantee that its measures are consistent with its principles. Ben & Jerry's has established a powerful image for ethical conduct by emphasizing societal duty and stakeholder involvement.

3. *Salesforce*: Salesforce is an established manufacturer of customer relationship management programs that are dedicated to business duty. The business has taken multiple initiatives to back ecological long-term viability, such as the use of green power in its data centres and it additionally places importance on diversity and inclusion in its staff. Furthermore, Salesforce is open about its attempts and cooperates with clients and staff to guarantee that its acts are consistent with its principles. Salesforce has established a powerful image for ethical conduct by organising business duties and stakeholder involvement.

These case studies show that by organising openness, responsibility and stakeholder involvement, businesses can effectively navigate ethical challenges. Businesses may establish trust and commitment with clients and staff and ensure ongoing sustainable development by adopting a strategic approach and organising stakeholder desires beyond brief economic advancement.

Part X

Global Trends and the Future of International Business Communication

27

Emerging Trends in Global Business Communication

Global business communication technological advances have advanced dramatically in the last decade. Instruments and communication patterns have transformed beyond e-mail and toward more approachable, intended methods of reaching staff members. It's critical to acknowledge these communication patterns since the capacity to grow and change is critical for businesses that desire to keep flourishing companies. The top emerging trends in global business communication are listed as follows:

Emerging Intranet Programs

Intranet programs, also known as electronic job-related solutions, are the most important business communication instruments used by successful businesses. Based on one research, 85% of businesses have a type of intranet or staff center. Businesses require a centrally managed location for accessing centrally managed material, data and individuals to function efficiently. The advantages of social networking sites, the advancement of cell phones and the development of remote employment have all contributed to this trend. An emerging intranet consolidates all of the interactions, records and individuals into a single, always-accessible location.

Modern intranet programs are person-centered, with acquainted societal characteristics, such as action streams, alerts, comments and likes, as well as websites, wikis and collaboration instruments.They also provide a more suitable means of communication, allowing everyone to communicate and share concepts from any place.

Cooperative Electronic Workplaces

Effective businesses understand the importance of teamwork in increasing output. As an outcome, intuitive cooperative electronic workplaces are a hot pattern in business communication.

Modern electronic workplaces enable staff to collaborate as if they were in the same space. Coediting records, sharing concepts, delegating activities and discovering data are all possible with a strong set of information administration instruments. It's become an essential function for numerous businesses since groups working in the same developing or across the country require workplaces to monitor advancement, centralise materials and individuals and remove unneeded e-mails that clog work processes.

Integrated Communication

Another business communication pattern to keep an eye on is integrated communication. The majority of staff nowadays anticipate a single origin of truth when it regards comprehending their objectives and performing their tasks effectively.

Staff are frequently dispersed across various systems, with overflowing inboxes. Internal communications program eliminates unread messages by consolidating essential statements, material and discussions in one location. This involves chat offerings, telephone and video conferences, messaging, and review and comment platforms. Staff also obtain data that is pertinent to them, which reduces ambiguity and offers a uniform user interface and expertise across a variety of gadgets and media. A cohesive communication structure minimises structure expenses and offers centralised characteristics for a more responsive encounter by connecting 3-way communications: managers to staff, staff to managers and staff with one another. It makes life easier for everyone and allows the administration to swiftly see when staff are accessible.

Robust Mobile Gadgets

Mobile is the undisputed monarch of business communication technological advances. Powerful smartphone applications offer the workplace to individuals, wherever they are—they are traveling to the workplace, attending a real-life meeting or on the go.

Staff can use mobile intranet applications to ping teammates, access business information and obtain essential alerts. This connection enables you to improve interpersonal interactions via your business.

Cloud-based Applications

Your business can access anything, anyplace by preserving business information in the cloud. Cloud-based resources and applications are also available on mobile equipment, making project collaboration and communication with the group much easier. Because of its adaptability, numerous businesses prefer cloud intranet software, which includes real-time modifying capacities and other developed sharing choices.

Seamless Technology Incorporation

The capacity to move interactions and information from a single system to another is so important these days that you don't even consider it. All gadgets are anticipated to sync discussions, operations and notes.

This business communication pattern can also be seen in certain BYOD efforts. Certain businesses motivate staff to use gadgets for both work and personal purposes, minimizing the hassle between the two. As it transforms out, the procedure greatly improves business communication.

Chat Services

Chat services provide an immediate and simple method for teammates to communicate without the need for lengthy e-mail processes. Not only do you get the data you require more quickly, but you are also able to employ a variety of media. You may also incorporate chat into your electronic job-related dynamics with the right intranet system (e.g., consider Axero's Slack Intranet Integration).

Numerous contemporary intranet responses such as Axero include built-in chat characteristics, allowing you to eliminate one platform. Intranet chat is available in real-time while staying discrete.

Video Communication

When it involves communication, digital media is the way to go—and it's an enormous company communication trend. You may render the material more interesting and absorbing for your staff by including pictures, videos and data visualizations.

Video is employed to train employees, demonstrate a procedure and disseminate important business notifications from the administration. Because video is more involved, it is more efficient as an internal communication medium, which is why more businesses are adopting it.

Infographics and Images

It's no secret the material with infographics and images is more engaging than plain text. As a result of this awareness, business communication dynamics include a suite of WYSIWYG releasing instruments to help you create content that is stimulating, nice and stands out to your staff.

These instruments enable you to incorporate infographics, vibrant images and illustrations that express content in a compelling manner. They are additionally extremely helpful in describing a procedure to staff members and there are numerous instruments and applications accessible to assist you in designing and creating them at an affordable price.

In essence, over the last decade, global business communication technology has undergone transformative changes, shifting from conventional e-mail to more user-friendly methods. Key trends include the prevalence of user-centric intranet programs, collaborative electronic workplaces fostering efficient teamwork, integrated communication systems providing a unified information source, robust mobile devices for remote engagement, the adoption of cloud-based applications enabling flexible data access, seamless technology integration, the emergence of chat services for direct communication, the growing significance of video, infographics and images in enhancing engagement and conveying information effectively. These trends highlight the importance of adaptability and efficiency in today's workplace.

Activity

1. In what ways have intranet programs transformed into crucial communication instruments for successful enterprises?
2. How does seamless data transfer between systems enhance business communication, particularly in BYOD initiatives encouraging dual-use of devices for work and personal purposes?
3. In what ways do effective smartphone applications enhance interpersonal interactions within the business environment?
4. How does the use of chat services contribute to establishing a prompt and effective communication avenue among team members?
5. How do infographics and visuals contribute to improving the understanding of processes and information among staff within an organization?
6. How does the utilization of cloud-based intranet software improve collaboration on projects and simplify communication among team members?

28

Impact of Globalisation and Technological Advancements

Globalisation has had an important effect on all societies. Economic expansion has been the main force of growth. Technology has accelerated globalisation and globalisation has consistently driven novel technologies ahead. Globalisation and technology are synonymous to each other. Globalisation has been significantly simplified by the advancement of digital technology. Advances in digital technology force businesses to become international since they require larger marketplaces to achieve finances of size. Advances in digital technology minimise cross-country travel and interaction expenses while also facilitating international procurement of basic supplies and other inputs. It promotes globalisation because the venture that owns the patent can abuse foreign markets with little rivalry. Digital technology is defined as electronic gadgets, structures and assets that aid in the creation, storage and management of data. Information Technology (IT), which relates to the application of computing devices for processing data and information, is a vital part of digital technology.

The Advancement of Communication and Technology

We identify 5 significant turning points in the history of communication:

- Owing to the development of writing, individuals are now capable to document occurrences and communicate.
- Mass-produced textual materials were made possible with the invention of printing in the 15th century, which allowed for the massive manufacturing of textbooks and other textual materials. Several important societal

transformations were carried about by this, such as the rise of newspapers and the expansion of reading and education.

- Instant person-to-person (P2P) interaction by electric power. Due to the creation of the electrical telegraph and the use of Morse protocol by telegraph workers, individuals could converse instantaneously at a range. This made it possible for the telephone to be created later;
- Instant mass media allowed for continuous broadcasting to a large population due to the invention of the radio and subsequently TV; and
- Communication made possible by technological advancements involving numerous, concurrent receivers and senders. Computers and individuals today interact with one another in a seamless manner.

The Transition from IT to ICT

The integration of the Online & the WWW is typically the foundation for the *data superhighway* concept that has captivated certain computer experts, not to mention influential governmental people too. Despite the fact that they are occasionally confused, these were not identical items. A network of networks (N2N) is the simplest way to describe the Online. It is the network of digital links that allows people to transmit and access data in different manners. The WWW, which we will henceforth refer to as the Web, is one among these methods.

From being a modest network of the US army and academic locations in the early 1960s, the Internet has expanded into a global N2N that shares a framework of protocols for sending and receiving content. For instance, 'HTTP' refers to Hypertext Transfer Protocol, a collection of protocols that enables the communication between networks and particular devices as well as the retrieval of documents from and uploading to websites.

Fundamentally described, a server is a machine that stores data that may be shared through a network and the Web. Various things are possible—thanks to other protocols. FTP, for instance, enables you to download a file onto the computer from a distant computer.

Because of technology, we are now able to converse in ways that seemed like science fiction just a couple of generations ago. For instance, with the home PC and the appropriate tools and connectivity, one can:

- Connect to other computers anywhere in the globe in a few minutes, while this timeline is frequently overly optimistic during peak moments;
- Download data from computers all around the globe;
- Send and receive e-mails to and from individuals worldwide;
- Peruse the data available in libraries and colleges around the world;
- Search databases worldwide;
- Engage in online gaming involving players from around the globe;
- Make the database publicly available such that anyone in the globe might conceivably access it;
- Retrieve and replay multimedia files, including video and audio recordings.

All of these resources are also accessible to any business, regardless of size. Additionally, business consumers can currently transact business online by selling commodities and activities (a practice known as e-commerce, which we'll discuss subsequently). For a while now, these services have indeed been accessible via the Internet. Yet these developments are based on several really old concepts. E-commerce encompasses a broad spectrum of activities, such as online retail, electronic payments, digital marketing and the secure transfer of information. The fundamental objective of e-commerce is to streamline and facilitate the exchange of products and services through digital means, offering convenience and efficiency to both sellers and buyers. It relies on various technologies and online platforms to create virtual marketplaces, enabling businesses to operate online storefronts and engage in secure and efficient online transactions.

In the realm of global business communication, the intersection of globalisation and technological progress has significantly transformed the landscape. Traditional communication barriers have collapsed, creating a borderless business environment characterised by instant connectivity. The incorporation of advanced technologies has not only expedited the exchange of information but has also fundamentally changed how businesses function globally. While this offers unprecedented opportunities for cross-cultural cooperation and market expansion, it requires a strategic approach to navigate potential challenges, such as cultural misunderstandings and information overload. In essence, the future of international business communication entails judiciously leveraging technology, adapting to diverse cultural contexts, and fostering a dynamic and inclusive collaboration approach in our interconnected world.

Activity

1. What are the five pivotal moments in the evolution of communication, and in what ways have they impacted society?
2. How has the Internet transformed from its humble beginnings as a limited network to a worldwide infrastructure with a protocol framework facilitating content exchange?
3. Explain HTTP and its function in facilitating communication between networks and devices, as well as in retrieving documents from websites.
4. How does e-commerce enable businesses of all sizes to access resources?
5. How does the integration of digital technology streamline the globalization endeavours of businesses, and what prompts its contribution to the expansion of internationalisation?
6. How has the intersection of globalization and technology transformed global business communication, and what challenges and opportunities does it present?

Bibliography

Abdin, M. D. (2008). The Barriers of Communication & Guidance of Effective Communication. *The Barriers of Communication & Guidance of Effective Communication (January 2008).*

Agarwal, M. (2007). *Business Communication.* Krishna Prakashan Media.

Al-Obaidani, K. (2015). *Ideological aspects of the translation of business annual reports in Oman (English-Arabic)* (Doctoral dissertation, Aston University).

Akter, N. (2016). Employee training and employee development are the predictors of employee performance; A study on garments manufacturing sector in Bangladesh. *IOSR Journal of Business and Management*, *18*(11), 48-57.

Ali, M. O. (2009). Business Communication: Theory & Application.

App, T. C., & Hub, T. C. A beginner's guide to business communication.

Aswathappa, K., & Reddy, G. S. (2009). *Organizational Behaviour* (Vol. 20). Mumbai: Himalaya Publishing House.

Bahl, J. C., & Nagamia, S. M. (1974). Modern Business Correspondence and Minute Writing.

Bardia, G. (2010). Smart Communication: The Key to Managing Your New Age Business. *IUP Journal of Soft Skills*, *4*(4).

Benjamin, J. B., & McKerrow, R. E. (1994). *Business and Professional Communication: Concepts and Practices*. Allyn & Bacon.

Bhatia, V. K., & Bremner, S. (2012). English for business communication. *Language teaching*, *45*(4), 410-445.

Bond, A. (2007). *300+ Successful Business Letters for All Occasions*. Barron's Educational Series.

Bosticco, M. (1988). *Instant Business Letters*. Gower Publishing Company, Limited.

Bovée, C. L. (2008). *Business Communication Today*. Pearson Education India.

Bradbury, A. J. (2006). *Successful Presentation Skills* (Vol. 111). Kogan Page Publishers.

Bremner, S. (2010). Collaborative writing: Bridging the gap between the textbook and the workplace. *English for Specific Purposes*, 29(2), 121-132.

Bushee, B. J., Core, J. E., Guay, W., & Hamm, S. J. (2010). The role of the business press as an information intermediary. *Journal of Accounting Research*, *48*(1), 1-19.

Carey, J. A. (Ed.). (2002). *Business letters for busy people: time-saving, ready-to-use letters for any occasion*. Red Wheel/Weiser.

Candee, A. M. (1920). *Business Letter Writing*. Biddle Publishing Company.

Casady, M., & Wasson, L. (1994). Written communication skills of international business persons. *The Bulletin of the Association for Business Communication*, 57(4), 36-40.

Chaturvedi, P. D. (2011). *Business Communication: Concepts, Cases, and Applications*. Pearson Education India.

Clark, C. (2008). The impact of entrepreneurs' oral 'pitch' presentation skills on business angels' initial screening investment decisions. *Venture Capital*, *10*(3), 257-279.

CL & Thill, B. JV (2014). Business Communication Today.

Cloke, M., & Wallace, R. (1969). *The Modern Business Letter Writer's Manual*. Doubleday.

Cooper, L., Orrell, J., & Bowden, M. (2010). *Work Integrated Learning: A Guide to Effective Practice*. Routledge.

Cosman, O. (2013). Written Communication in Business. *USV Annals of Economics & Public Administration*, *13*(1).

Cruthers, A. (2020). *Business writing for everyone*. Kwantlen Polytechnic University.

Ćurlin, T., Pejić Bach, M., & Miloloža, I. (2020). Presentation skills of business and economics students: Cluster analysis. *Croatian Review of Economic, Business and Social Statistics*, 6(2), 27-42.

Duica, M. C., Florea, N. V., & Duica, A. (2016). Improving Verbal Communication from the Perspective of the Use of Organizational Voice and Silence. *Annals of The University Dunarea De Jos Of Galati: Fascicle XVII, Medicine*, 22(2), 118-124.

Fay, M., & Williams, L. (1993). Gender bias and the availability of business loans. *Journal of Business Venturing*, *8*(4), 363-376.

Flatley, M. E. (1982). A comparative analysis of the written communication of managers at various organizational levels in the private business sector. *The Journal of Business Communication (1973)*, *19*(3), 35-49.

Florea, N. V. (2014). Implementing a model of strategic communication to obtain organizational performance. *Land Forces Academy Review*, *19*(3), 256.

Gopal, N. (2009). *Business Communication*. New Age International.

Guffey, M. E., & Loewy, D. (2014). *Business Communication: Process and product*. Cengage Learning.

Guffey, M. E., & Loewy, D. (2015). *Essentials of Business Communication*. Cengage Learning.

Guffey, M. E., & Loewy, D. (2022). *Essentials of business communication*. Cengage Learning.

Halpern, J. W., Kilborn, J. M., & Lokke, A. M. (1988). *Business Writing: Strategies and Samples*. New York: Macmillan.

Hamilton, C. (2013). *Communicating for Results: A Guide for Business and the Professions*. Cengage Learning.

Hamilton, P. J. Process of Business Communication and Barriers of Business Communication.

Harcourt, J., Krizan, A. C., & Merrier, P. (1991). *Business Communication*. South-Western.

Hargie, O. (2021). *Skilled interpersonal communication: Research, Theory, and Practice*. Routledge.

Himstreet, W. C., & Baty, W. M. (1981). *Business Communications: Principles and Methods*. Brooks/Cole.

Ibay, S. B., & Pa-also, M. A. C. (2020). An Assessment of the Managerial Skills and Professional Development Needs of Private Catholic Secondary School Administrators in Bangkok, Thailand. *World Journal of Education*, *10*(1), 149-163.

Jayasree, M., & Ragini, G. Communication Skills in Employability Opportunities.

Katte, A. Y., & Joshi, A. D. (2019). Recent trends in business communication. 74.

Kincaid, H. V., & Bright, M. (1957). Interviewing the business elite. *American Journal of Sociology*, *63*(3), 304-311.

Kumar, R. (2010). *Basic Business Communication*. Excel Books India.

Kumbhar, V. M. (2013). Business communications. *SSRN Electronic Journal*.

Kyeyune, D., & Delilah, D. (2020). Answers to Essentials of Business Communication by Mary Ellen Guffey and Dana Loewy. *Available at SSRN 3621368*.

Lindsell-Roberts, S. (2004). *Strategic Business Letters and E-mails*. Houghton Mifflin Harcourt.

Mayfield, M., Mayfield, J., & Walker, R. (2020). Fundamental theories of Business Communication. *Laying a Foundation for the Field*.

McBride, N. (2016). *Intervention research: a practical guide for developing evidence-based school prevention programs*. Springer.

McCarthy, G. (2010). Approaches to the postgraduate education of business coaches. *Australian Journal of Adult Learning*, *50*(2), 323-357.

McLean, S. (2010). *Business Communication for Success*. Boston, MA: Flat World Knowledge.

Murdick, W. (1998). *The Portable Business Writer*. Houghton Mifflin College Division.

Neuliep, J. W. Intercultural Communication. A contextual approach, (2003).

Nystrand, M. (1983). The role of context in written communication. *The Nottingham Linguistic Circular*, *12*(1), 55-65.

Palmer, I., Dunford, R., & Buchanan, D. (2016). *EBOOK: Managing Organizational Change: A Multiple Perspectives Approach (ISE)*. McGraw Hill.

Polonskya, M. J., & Wallerb, D. S. (2004). Making oral presentations: Some practical guidelines and suggestions. *The Marketing Review*, *4*(4), 431-444.

Prabavathi, R., & Nagasubramani, P. C. (2018). Effective oral and written communication. *Journal of Applied and Advanced Research*, *3*(1), 29-32.

Ramachandran, K. K., Lakshmi, K. K., & Kumar, M. K. (2007). *Business Communication*. Macmillan.

Rao, P. S. (2008). *Management and Organisational Behaviour (text, Cases & Games)*. Himalaya Publishing House.

Rudansky-Kloppers, S. (2002). *Business Communication: In Perspective*. New Africa Books.

Schaub, M., & McClure, H. (2020). Flipping the Script: Students as Authors of an Open-Access Business Communication Textbook. *Engaging Students through Campus Libraries: High-Impact Learning Models*, 65.

Shitel, M. O., & Suprun, O. (2019). Effective business communication is a core element of business management.

Sigband, N. B. (1965). Other worlds to conquer. *Journal of Business Communication*, 2(2), 29-38.

Sova, D. B. (2002). *How to write articles for newspapers and magazines*. Arco.

Tambade, S. A. Recent Trends and Transitory Nature of Business Communication.

Taylor, S. (2004). *Model Business Letters, E-mails & Other Business Documents, 6/e*. Pearson Education India.

Taylor, T., Doherty, A., & McGraw, P. (2015). *Managing People in Sports Organizations: A Strategic Human Resource Management Perspective*. Routledge.

Toth, C. (2013). Revisiting a genre: Teaching infographics in business and professional communication courses. *Business Communication Quarterly*, 76(4), 446-457.

Valentina, F. N., & Antoaneta, T. I. (2016). Improving communication with the internal public and customers of an industrial company: a major challenge along the supply chain. In *Supply Chain Strategies and the Engineer-to-Order Approach* (pp. 17-42). IGI Global.

Wienbroer, D., Hughes, E., & Silverman, J. (2010). *Rules of Thumb for Business Writers*. McGraw Hill Professional.

Young, P. H. (1994). *Electronic Communication Techniques*. Merrill.